Caroline Thon

Armenians in Hamburg

l i n e s

Beiträge zur Stadtforschung
aus dem Institut für Ethnologie
der Universität Hamburg

herausgegeben von

Waltraud Kokot

Band 8

LIT

Caroline Thon

Armenians in Hamburg

An ethnographic exploration into the relationship between diaspora and success

LIT

Cover photo by Caroline Thon

Gedruckt auf alterungsbeständigem Werkdruckpapier entsprechend
ANSI Z3948 DIN ISO 9706

Bibliographic information published by the Deutsche Nationalbibliothek
The Deutsche Nationalbibliothek lists this publication in the Deutsche Nationalbibliografie; detailed bibliographic data are available in the Internet at http://dnb.d-nb.de.

A catalogue record for this book is available from the British Library

Klosbachstr. 107
CH-8032 Zürich
Tel. +41 (0) 44-251 75 05
Fax +41 (0) 44-251 75 06
e-Mail: zuerich@lit-verlag.ch
http://www.lit-verlag.ch

LIT VERLAG Dr. W. Hopf
Berlin 2012
Fresnostr. 2
D-48159 Münster
Tel. +49 (0) 2 51-620 320
Fax +49 (0) 2 51-23 19 72
e-Mail: lit@lit-verlag.de
http://www.lit-verlag.de

Distribution:

In Germany: LIT Verlag Fresnostr. 2, D-48159 Münster
Tel. +49 (0) 2 51-620 32 22, Fax +49 (0) 2 51-922 60 99, e-mail: vertrieb@lit-verlag.de

In Austria: Medienlogistik Pichler-ÖBZ, e-mail: mlo@medien-logistik.at

In Switzerland: B + M Buch- und Medienvertrieb, e-mail: order@buch-medien.ch

In the UK: Global Book Marketing, e-mail: mo@centralbooks.com

Table of Contents

Acknowledgements

When doing their work cultural anthropologists are always dependent on several variables e.g. a well-defined research question and its operationalisation, proper methods end evaluation tools, money and time to spend etc. Still the most important factor is the one which is least foreseeable and manipulable: That is your informants i.e. the people who make your research a success.

Therefore I am deeply in debt towards my Armenian acquaintances who spent their valuable time on answering my questions and telling me their personal life stories, who gave me advise, who accompanied me through the whole research phase and who trusted me. Besides nourishing my research, they provided me with exciting and moving insights into the history and the presence of Armenian life in the diaspora. By publicising my research results I hope to pay back a tiny bit of the effort, which those people made to make my thesis possible. Thanks a million!

Also, I also want to thank my student colleagues who were involved in the same research project and gave me valuable support and took time to discuss my thesis. My thanks also go to Tatevik Ayvazyan, a brilliant young Armenian woman, who often accompanied me in the field and made the research even more pleasant and insightful. Finally, I want to thank Prof. Dr. Waltraud Kokot who initiated and supervised the research project, encouraged me and who gave me the opportunity to make my results public

1 Introduction

This publication is a revised and shortened version of my Master thesis on the Armenian diaspora community in Hamburg, which I produced in 2008. It is grounded on empirical data which was collected in the context of an ongoing comparative European research project on diaspora communities and their relation to success. The project called DiaspoRes[1] was launched by Prof. Waltraud Kokot of the Institute of Social and Cultural Anthropology of the University in Hamburg in cooperation with further academic institutes in diverse European cities[2] in 2006. The idea for the project stems from the observation that certain diasporas, historically as well as recently, seem to be particularly "successful" in their host societies. By comparative research on diverse diaspora communities in European cities, major factors of diasporic success shall be discerned as well as specific resources that diasporas provide for their members in this regard. Diasporic success is thereby not understood or examined as an essential feature of a certain ethnic diasporic group. Thus, the statement is not that one group is more successful than the other "by nature". Rather success of a group is understood to be a product of and to be dependent on the group's resources and cultural strategies as well as external factors i.e. the host society's political, economic, and social conditions (Kokot 2007b).

Within the framework of this project I conducted fieldwork in the Armenian diaspora community in Hamburg in 2007/2008. Exploring the Armenian community was a particularly interesting undertaking as it is one of the oldest diasporas in the world and, at the same time, almost unknown to the German public. The general invisibility of the Armenians as an ethnic group is alluded to by the cover picture: Here, you St. Gertrud's church in Hamburg, a conventional Protestant church in Northern Germany (photo by C. Thon). One would hardly ever expect

[1] The acronym DiaspoRes stands for „Diaspora as a Resource".
[2] Sofia, Bulgaria; Copenhagen, Denmark; Fribourg, Switzerland; London, Great Britain; Amsterdam, the Netherlands and Thessalonica, Greece.

that this church is also used by the Armenian community for religious practice. But it is. This cooperative usage of ecclesiastical edifices is not a singular case but almost normal to Armenian communities in Germany. Though Armenian life and practice exist they remain invisible to most of us. Apart from the lack of Armenian traces in the public, the Armenians in Germany have been only rarely a subject of ethnographic or other research.[3] In contrast, other countries of residence are well aware of the existence of the Armenian diaspora and their historical fate.

I consider my research a first exploration into the relation of diaspora and success in the Armenian community in Hamburg. It was led by the overarching questions, whether life in the diaspora encourages the development of specific concepts or strategies of success – and, if so, what are the specific resources of the diaspora that enable these strategies? These questions certainly can only be answered from the final comparative perspective which the project aims to establish. But in order to make a first approach to these complex questions I set the main focus of my study on the investigation of the cultural concept of success: My aim was to detect consensual norms, values and strategies, which are bound to the Armenians' notion of success and which, thus, promote or hinder agency for success of the examined group and its individuals in the host society. That means that the term "success" appears in this research in two different ways: firstly, in the context of a specific cognitive concept among the members of the diaspora, which is culturally bound – the emic[4] notion of success; secondly, it is applied as an etic[5] category of analysis with the objective to determine whether the group

---

[3] Research on contemporary issues concerning Armenians in Germany is conducted only by few Armenian and non-Armenian scholars in Germany, for example, Tessa Hofmann (1997a; 2005), Mihran Dabag (1994; 1995), Azat Ordukhanyan (2005), Andrea Tauber (1999).

[4] The ethnographic term "emic" implies that a socio-cultural phenomenon is understood and interpreted from the perspective of the examined individual or group (Hirschberg 1988: 116). An ethnographer thus duplicates the perception of his informants and discerns their cognitive categories and semantics.

[5] "Etic" – being the antonym of „emic" – denotes the view from the outside on a socio-cultural phenomenon (Hirschberg 1988: 116). In this case, categories of understanding are those of the external observer, the researcher him- or herself.

can be judged as successful from the external perspective. With regard to the latter usage of the term "success" Bourdieu's capital forms – social, cultural, economic and symbolic capital - were chosen as a theoretical backbone: The etic term "success" was thus operationalized as the accumulation and mutual transformation of cultural, social and economic capital, which eventually enable the participation in economically and/or politically significant decisions and the gain of wealth as well as prestige. It further showed during the evaluation of my data that Bourdieu's concept of the habitus was valuable to understand how Armenians perceived themselves and heterogeneity inside their group concerning life in the diaspora and the meaning of and the striving for success. Therefore I included an excursus on this issue.

As the case study on the Armenian community in Hamburg is just a blink in the Armenian diaspora and its history I will give an overview over the broader historical background of the diaspora. Furthermore, I will embed my research on "success and diaspora" and give an idea of the external factors, which influence the life of the Armenian community in Hamburg and may also determine the capacity of the group to become successful: E.g. the broader context of the Armenian diaspora community in Germany, the (legal) circumstances of migration. I will also shed some light on the economic strategies and the institutionalized social networks of the Armenians in Hamburg.

Finally, this study is primarily to be understood as a first heuristic exploration that delivers material for the further formulation of hypotheses on the relation of "success" and "diaspora". The amount of data which I collected by reviewing literature and by doing empirical research is not sufficient to bring about final conclusions on my research topic or the life of the Armenian diaspora community in Hamburg. Rather its purpose is to lay a foundation for further field studies on this scientific desideratum.

Remarks: 1. The transliteration of Armenian expressions in German and English literature is not standardized. This is due to the existence of two Armenian dialects - Eastern and Western Armenian - and their diverse transliterations in the different sources.
2. Most interviews were conducted in German. In order improve the readability of the text I translated German interview quotes into English.

1.1 Key concepts

What do I mean when talking about "diaspora"? And what is Bourdieu's theory of "capital" and his term "habitus" about? Before plunging into the facts and the history of the Armenian diaspora I will shortly clarify the central terms of my research in order to prepare a common ground of understanding.

Diaspora

The term "diaspora" derives from the Greek "diaspeirein" meaning "to scatter" (Tölölyan 1996: 9). Having become a salient concept in Social and Cultural Science debates since the 1990s, scholars fervently argue about the definition boundaries of diaspora – which thereby roughly stretch from a semantic field embracing a plurality of phenomena of human mobility in the globalized age (Tölölyan 1991: 4) to a narrow notion of a people having been dispersed, thus leaning to the paradigmatic diasporic history of the Jews (Safran 2004: 9-10).

In order to define "diaspora" I will depart from this general debate as I am primarily interested in diaspora as a concrete social form, which expresses itself in a distinct culture and structural organization (Cohen 1971: 267; Vertovec 1997: 257 -258). The oft-preferred contemplation of diaspora as a "type of consciousness", meaning a community built up by identity discourse, will be of secondary interest (Oussatcheva 2001: 7; Schwalgin&Sökefeld 2000: 3; Vertovec 1997: 281f.). Under these premises the existence of diaspora is not a question of the conditions or trigger of dispersion, but an empirical question: As Marienstras comments the passing of time shows whether a migrant or exilic group constitutes the social form and consciousness of diaspora (Marienstras 1989: 125). As an objective indicator for a manifestation of a diaspora as a social form, I will take the existence of specific diasporic institutions (see also Oussatcheva 2001: 7). This aspect of institutionalized community emphasizes the importance of the local rootedness and *Vergemeinschaftung* of diaspora in its country of residence and rules out groups who resemble diasporas in respect to their transnational activity (see Glick-Schiller et al. 1995: 50f.; see Kokot et al. 2004: 5).

Borrowing from the concepts of diaspora by several scholars (Schwalgin& Sökefeld 2000: 2; Vertovec 1997: 278-279) and taking into account the above mentioned line of thought the working definition of diaspora here is based on:

- the voluntary or coerced dispersion of a group from the country which is considered their homeland to more than one country
- the establishment of triadic transnational relations (imagined or practised) between the homeland, the country of residence and among the diaspora communities themselves
- the maintenance of a collective identity
- the building of institutions that serve the discursive and practical reproduction of the diaspora community and its identity, and thus also
- a certain degree of communication and interaction among the individuals of a community

The Armenian diaspora community – as will implicitly be proven in my further writing – complies with these criteria.

Bourdieu's theory of capital and the concept of habitus

Capitals are resources. The accumulation, possession and staking of capital in the social environment determines one's ability to participate in and influence one's social environment, and, thus, to gain and execute power (Bourdieu& Wacquant 1996: 128). Bourdieu distinguishes four major forms of capital – economic, cultural, social and symbolic - which have different qualities and offer different chances of participation; they can be transformed into each other under acknowledgement of their specific quality and the valid exchange rate, which is determined by the existent power relations of capital holders (ibid. 1996: 128-129, 151). Nevertheless, the effectiveness of capital i.e. the social, economic and cultural resources one holds, cannot be taken for granted. It always depends on the social recognition of the capital of the individual as "legitimate" (see below) and whether its holder is allowed to enter the "market" of a given group or not (ibid. 1996: 128, 130, 139). This notion is also important to consider when analyzing the effectiveness and convertibility of the capital "imported" by migrants into their new society of residence.

Cultural capital exists in different states[1]. First, it takes the form of embodied capital being defined as "cultivation", a complex of diverse cultural competences (e.g. manners, language, knowledge etc.), which the individual acquires via informal and formal education (Bourdieu 1982: 120-121; 2005: 55). Therefore, cultural capital is accumulated by "learning" and is inscribed into the individual's social body, i.e. it becomes part of its habitus (see below) (Bourdieu 2005: 56). The primary and most important place of transmission and appropriation of embodied cultural capital is the family: Here - depending on the prevalence of accumulated cultural capital in the family - the individual may gain cultural capital during its socialization via "inheritance", a process, whose economic character as a resource remains mostly opaque (ibid. 2005: 54, 58). The secondary acquisition of cultural capital is realized in the formalized institutions of education (school, university etc.). Here, acquired cultural capital can also gain the state of institutionalized capital by taking the shape of certificates of educational attainments (academic titles etc.). That effectively means that one's cultural competences are

[1] I will only refer to the embodied and institutionalized form of cultural capital as relevant dimensions.

legitimized, i.e. socially recognized, and their convertibility into economic and symbolic capital is strengthened (ibid. 2005: 74).

Social capital can be understood as the potential economic, cultural and symbolic capital that is accessible to an individual or group by its social network being defined as the total of all existent and virtual, mutually recognized relations, which can be mobilized (Bourdieu&Wacquant 1996: 152). Depending on the totality of capital of its members, a social network has a multiplying effect on the capitals of the individual (Bourdieu 2005: 64). Though social capital basically relies on the belonging to a group it can be institutionalized (marriage, membership in parties, clubs etc.); still its institutionalized form demands constant work as the individual has to invigorate the relations every now and then (ibid. 2005: 63-65). Most easy to circumscribe are the boundaries of economic capital: It comprises all material goods which can be converted into money; economic capital gains institutionalized shape when it appears in the form of property (ibid. 2005: 52).

Though Bourdieu in general negates a stable structural hierarchy between the social, cultural and economic capital regarding their importance, he admits that the accumulation of economic capital tends to be most important in a free market system, where the economic field is dominant (ibid. 1996: 140-141; Bourdieu 1985: 11). Nevertheless, the accumulation of economic capital can hardly be judged as a "success" if it goes without social recognition. Thus, from an etic point of view the ability to accumulate economic capital and transform it into symbolic capital tends to be most important regarding success.

Symbolic capital thereby is based on the act of social recognition. It can be translated as "prestige" or "reputation". Actually it is not a capital by itself but it is inherent in the social, economic or cultural capital whenever these are perceived in their respective fields[2] of logic; there, a surplus may result in special distinction

[2] As the "open terms" by Bourdieu refuse brief definitions see Bourdieu&Wacquant (1996: 126-131) for the term "field".

(e.g. a “summa cum laude” in university) (Bourdieu&Wacquant 1996: 151; Bourdieu 2005: 57). Symbolic capital is also *per se* inherent in social relations as they, by definition, rely on mutual social recognition (Bourdieu 2005: 77). Symbolic capital gains a more manifest and lasting character when it is, for example, a product of seemingly altruistic investment of economic capital into the common good, i.e. benevolent or philanthropic commitment (ibid. 1987: 245).

Finally, Bourdieu’s term of “habitus”: The habitus can be understood as a system of structured and structuring dispositions, which are embodied by the individual by education (and thus also reproducing the dispositions, which are bound to familial social provenance) and its interaction with the social environment (Bourdieu &Wacquant 1996: 129, 160). The dispositions are inherent in the social body as schemes of values, perception and agency and thus determine the scope of an individual’s social and cultural practice and its interpretation of the social world (Bourdieu&Wacquant 1996: 160, 162; Bourdieu 1987: 98). As such, the habitus expresses itself in the form of one’s taste, aesthetic preferences, style, manners etc. (Bourdieu 1982: 25). Being based on experience, which is also determined by one’s position in the larger social system, and therefore by one’s adherence to a certain social stratum the habitus also refers to the dispositions, which are perceived as typical for a larger collective (ibid. 1987: 112). Thus, the ascription of a habitus to an individual also bears references to the “social class” with which he or she is associated.

2 The Armenian diaspora – Background information

In scientific discourse the Armenian diaspora - together with the Jewish diaspora - is considered the paradigmatic example of a diaspora (Safran 2004: 11). Its first dispersals can be traced back to 100 BC (Dekmejian 1997: 424). In the course of Armenian history diasporization and life in the diaspora have shown a greater continuity than independent statehood[1] (see Hofmann 1993: 12). During the long time spans of absence of a territorially defined political entity the diaspora was the only space for the maintenance of Armenian life. Since the 15th century the diaspora developed itself into the genuine motor of the Armenians' cultural and economic progress (Hofmann 1997b: 63). In the course of its existence it developed several institutions, which by acting on the transnational and the local level of the Armenian diaspora enabled its practical and ideological formation and maintenance. The main institutions to be mentioned are the Armenian Apostolic Church, which is after 1700 years of existence still the main shelter of the diaspora community; the so-called Diaspora parties, in particular, the rivalling socialist-nationalist Armenian Revolutionary Federation (*Dashnakzutyun*, abbr.: *Dashnak*) and the liberal-democratic *Ramgavar*, which were founded in 1890 in Tbilisi and 1921 in Constantinople respectively; the philanthropic organizations, the local cultural associations and the press and print media as well as educational institutions (Tölölyan 2000: 118; Hofmann 1993: 96-97; ibid. 1997a: 47; Dekmejian 1997: 424).

[1] The first kingdom Urartu, which is associated with the early Armenians, existed from the 9th to the 6th century BC (Redgate 1998: 5). Kingdoms of Armenian royal dynasties followed: The Erevanids (570–2nd century BC), the Artashesian dynasty (191-12 BC), the Arshakuni (53-287/428 AD), the Bagratids (862-1045 AD) and the Rubenids (1080-1375 AD) (Hofmann 1993: 12). Thereby it must be mentioned that only in the times of Tigran II Artschjan (95-55 BC) the whole historical area of Armenian settlement was united under Armenian reign (Hofmann 2005: 10).

After more than 500 years of statelessness the first Armenian Republic was constituted in 1918 comprising a small fraction of the lands[2], which are labelled the Armenian homeland (Hofmann 1993: 9). The independence of the First Republic was short-lived as it was incorporated into the Soviet Union in 1921. With the collapse of the Soviet Union it regained its independence in 1991. Presently, 18 years after the establishment of the independent Republic of Armenia, the diaspora still plays an eminent role; its existence is now justified by its enormous support of the young state in the shape of humanitarian and developmental aid by diaspora funds as well as the private remittances by the emigrants (Hofmann 1997b: 166; Strasser 2005: 153-154; Manaseryan 2004: 1f.): According to the National Statistics Service of the Republic of Armenia, remittances made up 10% of Armenia's GDP in 2003. In the same year about 60% of the remittances[3] stemmed from the diaspora, probably mostly from the so-called "New Diaspora", which is constituted by migrants from the Republic of Armenia (Roberts&Banaian 2004: 7, 15).

During the times of the Cold War relations between the diaspora and the Republic as well as between the diasporic parties were extremely strained (see Tölölyan 2000: 120-121; Panossian 1998: 157f.). The question of recognition of the Soviet Republic of Armenia as a homeland divided the communities into their tiniest ramifications – regarding their organizational as well as private life. Fault lines first showed between the Diaspora parties and their affiliates, here namely the political camp of the Dashnak and the other parties, which opposed as anti-Dashnak. This divide also affected the Armenian Apostolic Church (Dekmejian 1997:

---

[2] The historical area of Armenian settlement was about 400,000 square km, which is divided into *Armenia major* in the East and *Armenia minor* in the West. It stretched over the modern Republic of Armenia as well as parts of today's Azerbaijan, a huge part of Eastern Turkey, Southern Georgia and the northern peaks of Iraq and Iran (Hofmann 1993: 9).

[3] The National Statistical Service of the Republic of Armenia differentiates between seasonal workers who are non-emigrants, emigrant workers who have been abroad more than one but less than two years and Armenians living in the diaspora i.e. those who have been outside of Armenia for more than two years (Roberts&Banaian 2004: 6). Hence, the other 40% of remittances come from seasonal workers and emigrant workers.

415-416). It resulted in the creation of two segregated diasporas with their own structure:

> "There were two sets of umbrella organizations with global networks, linking the various branches of each bloc scattered in many countries. This meant there existed two parallel Armenian Apostolic Churches and two sets of cultural organizations, philanthropic societies, sports clubs, school systems, media outlets, and so forth. Socialization and intermarriage between the two blocs were rare." (Panossian 1998: 157)

Today, relations between the rivalling factions tend to relax and also the relation between the diaspora and the homeland is gradually being turned into an institutionalized cooperation now: In 1998, for example, the Diaspora Conference was established. During the first conventions in 1999 and 2002, representatives of Armenia and the diaspora communities gathered for concerting collaboration between Armenia and the diaspora (see Tölölyan 2000: 123-124). Since 1999 Armenia and the global diaspora communities have arranged a common sports event, the Pan-Armenian Games. Furthermore, the legal reform in 2007 on dual citizenship implicitly confirms the acceptance of a co-existence and interaction of an Armenian state and a diaspora (Ministry of Foreign Affairs of Republic of Armenia n. y.: 4). Tölölyan also diagnoses an on-going change in the Armenian diasporic consciousness: The self-image of the Armenian diaspora as a "nation-in-exile", in which the diasporic situation is seen as a temporary and unwanted state to be abandoned by final repatriation, tends to get substituted by a growing self-perception as a diasporic transnation which acknowledges the permanence of the diasporic phenomenon (Tölölyan 2000: 107-108).

Continuity of the diaspora over more than 2000 years as such does not exclude the fact that Armenian diaspora communities were and still are subordinated to their own life cycles, to "genesis, development, and extinction" (Dekmejian 1997: 413). Moreover, in the course of time Armenian diasporic migration has become multi-faceted and diasporic communities often multi-layered: In many cases, migration would not start from the Armenian homeland, but from settlements in the diaspora, and several existing communities were built up by different waves of migration of diverse origins. Thus, Armenians often experienced multiple relocations (Aghanian 2007: 4). Although the catastrophe of the genocide in Armenian history is perceived as *the* trigger of Armenian diasporization and serves as the nucleus of diasporic identity (Kokot&Dorsch 2006: 28) migrations were triggered by diverse events and followed different motives: Coercive factors had been economic crises and deprivations, political instability, conquest, religious persecution, massacres and deportations, while a motor of voluntary migration had been trade, the seeking of educational opportunities as well as military careers as mercenaries (Dekmejian 1997: 413). Several authors also emphasise the shaping influence and context of the host society on the development of community types (Dekmejian 1997: 413; Aghanian 2007: 5). Just considering these facts it is hard to keep the notion of static and monolithic diaspora or diaspora communities with clearly depicted boundaries and internal social, economic and cultural homogeneity.

2.1 Diasporization and community types

Though the Armenian diaspora cannot be imagined as a homogeneous entity the communities share certain traits concerning the cause of migration or dispersion and, therefore, are often categorised into two different types: Victim diaspora and trade diaspora communities. These categories stem from Robin Cohen's classification of diasporas. Among others, he identifies victim diasporas, which are constituted by migration on the ground of calamity or force, and trade diasporas, which are ethnic networks built up by voluntary migration following commercial pursuit (Cohen 1997: 23-24). But, as Aslanian as well as Kokot and Dorsch state, in the course of history Armenians not only constituted either victim diasporas or trade diasporas, but often one type evolved out of the other[4] (Aslanian 2004: 41;

[4] The blurring of Cohen's categories in reality also points to the fact that they are not suitable as analytic categories as they are not based on a strict systematic scheme of classification. Rather

Kokot&Dorsch 2006: 20-21). In their historical diaspora communities e.g. in the Middle East the Armenians often are said to have established themselves as a middleman minority (Bakalian 1994: 53; Hofmann 1993: 105-106; Christopher 1975: 273; Kouymjian 1997: 11) - although the dimension of this phenomenon is arguable (Walker 1988: 23; see also Lang&Walker 1991a: 17). The concept of middleman minorities is thereby generally associated with a minority's "intermediate" position in their host society. This intermediate position is manifest in their economic role being often mediators between different social or economic layers or busy in trade and commerce. Historically, the social position of middleman minorities is a precarious one, which is often met by hostility by the host society (Bonacich 1973: 583-584, 859). According to Bonacich middleman minorities share certain characteristics: They have a sojourner mentality; they prefer occupation which is of mobile or "liquid" character; they practise thrift and accept the delay of gratification; they tend to build cultural and territorial enclaves and live in segregation; they prefer the utilisation of ties built on familial, linguistic, regional and ethnic commonalities in the economic sphere (ibid. 1973: 584-589).

To what extent the Armenian communities complied or comply with all these criteria by Bonacich cannot be ascertained here. In terms of societal rank, the Armenian middlemanship was especially confirmed for the urban environments of Muslim Middle Eastern cities where Armenians took over the trading and financial sector as these activities were prohibited to Muslims (Hofmann 1993: 105-106). Also, they occupied technical and entrepreneurial roles, which had not been filled in the developing countries of the Middle East yet (Dekmejian 1997: 425), thus building ethnic economic niches. In those countries Armenian traders functioned as interfaces for European merchants as well as intermediaries between Christians and Jews, but they also acted as diplomatic mediators between the European and the indigenous authorities (Christopher 1975: 273; Dekmejian 1997: 425). Albeit the different contextual conditions, which exist in predominantly

they help to provide a very rough idea of the "nature" of the diaspora – and may serve as terminology for the different ways diasporas are perceived.

Christian or rather secular and modern societies, Bakalian states that the Armenians of New Jersey and New York also nowadays fit "to some extent" to Bonacich's middleman minority concept due to the high rate of self-employment, which Bakalian identifies as an "ethnic trait" and which can be considered a "mobile" occupation according to Bonacich (Bakalian 1994: 77; Bonacich 1973: 585). Further investigations on the diasporas in mainly secular and post-modern societies have to show whether a middleman position can be ascertained for the Armenians.

A distinctive feature of Armenian communities is their enormous upward mobility. Their economic success is mentioned in several accounts. Especially the Western Armenian diaspora communities, which are the result of the genocide, are said to have experienced a "bourgeoisification" in recent times (Tölölyan 2000: 115). The social ascent for example in the USA, Lebanon or France was managed in one to three generations (Boudjikanian 1988: 241; Mirak 1988: 180-181; Ter Minassian 1988: 213; Bakalian 1994: 8). Today, descriptions of the socio-economic character of Armenians in the diaspora range from as "generally middle-class", "middle-class professionals and business persons" to "upper-middle-class" minority (Aghanian 2007: 2; Bakalian 1994: 8; Talai 1986: 254; O'Grady 1981: 76). Thus, from an etic perspective, Armenian communities are in general perceived as successful in socio-economic terms.

According to many scholars, the early dispersions of the Armenians as victim and/ or trade diaspora were due to the geographical location of historical Armenia on the crossing of several trade routes, and its geo-strategically interesting character for the neighbouring empires (Hofmann 1993: 9, 12; Tölölyan 2000: 166; Redgate 1998: 10; Baladouni 1998: XVI). It was Persia – and since 1827 also the Russian Tsarist Empire – as neighbours in the East, Byzantium, Rome and the Ottoman Empire in the West, and the Mongols and Turks from Central Asia who caused calamities in Armenia by repetitive invasions and conquests (Hofmann 1993: 12; Tölölyan 2000: 166). Deportations and exodus during the last 1700 years spread Armenians especially into the Middle Eastern region, the Caucasus as well as the Balkan Peninsula and Southeast and East Europe (Hofmann 1993:

27, 30, 83; Aslanian 2004: 41). Merchant activities and the establishment of trading networks in the 17th century resulted in further dispersion reaching from Amsterdam in the West as far as to Guangdong (China), Mughal (India) and Manila (Philippines) in the East (Aslanian 2004: 43-44; Baladouni 1998: XVI-XVII).

Significant migration to the Western hemisphere and the transatlantic region occurred later in the late 19th century and was due to a chain of persecutions and massacres, which started with the pogroms against the Western Armenians under Sultan Abdulhamid II in the Ottoman Empire in 1894-96 and escalated into the later genocide under the Young Turks, which had its peak in 1915 to 1916 (Mirak 1988: 180). The event of the genocide still defines the intra-Armenian primary perception as a victim diaspora[5] (see Kokot&Dorsch 2006: 28).

Today, the shrinking or dissolution of older diasporic communities in the Middle East (e.g. Iran, Libya, Syria, Egypt, and Iraq) in favour of a migration to the younger settlements in the West is the prevailing tendency (Avagian 1994: 76). Reasons are political unrest and conflicts which shook the Middle East: Events like the occupation of Northern Cyprus by the Turks in 1974, the civil war in Lebanon (1958 and 1975-1990) and the Islamic Revolution in Iran 1979 caused Armenians to leave their settlements there (Redgate 1998: 275). New Armenian colonies are developing in New Zealand, Australia and many European countries (Avagian 1994: 76). However, the biggest exodus in Armenian history has been observed since the beginning of the 1990s as a consequence of the collapse of the USSR and the independence of the Third Republic of Armenia (Hofmann 2005: 16). Since the founding of the independent Republic of Armenia, its population has shrunk immensely: Unofficial estimations state that half of the former 3.7

---

[5] This also is expressed in the linguistic labelling. As Abrahamian points out, Armenian scholars agree that only the dispersion caused by the genocide is to be named "diaspora": "However, the genocide is such a strong marking point of the Armenian diaspora that Armenian scholars, as a rule, use the word *sp'yur'k'*, the equivalent of diaspora, only for the (greater) part of the diaspora formed as a result of the genocide in 1915, while all the other constituents, of both ancient and modern times, are called *gaght'ojakh* or *gaght'avayr* (lit. 'center' or 'place of resettlement')." (Abrahamian 2006: 329).

million inhabitants have left since 1991 (Strasser 2005: 153). Several crises, namely the war versus Azerbaijan over Nagorno-Karabakh (Arm.: *Arzach*), the disastrous earthquake in 1988 and the energy crisis that left Armenia almost without any electricity from 1992 to 1996 as well as economic insecurity have caused emigration. This movement can best be described as a brain drain as most migrants – legal and illegal – are well-educated[6] (Ishkanian 2002: 390). Since 1988 Russia, which had hosted historically old, but small Armenian communities for several centuries, has turned into an important destination of Armenian labour migration (Hofmann 2005: 17; Ishkanian 2002: 391; Hofmann 1997b: 167). Other destinations are the United States and European countries (Ritter 2007: 36). Thereby the prior existence of diaspora communities has, as Ishkanian points out, "facilitated, normalized, and, to a great extent, shaped the nature of post-Soviet Armenian emigration" as they served as nodes of destination for chain migration (Ishkanian 2002: 386-387).

Accurate figures of Armenian worldwide population are hardly available as national census is often based on nationality (Avagian 1994: 74-75). Estimations of the size of the Armenian diaspora in its global dimension differ depending on the source: Recent estimations by Tölölyan range from approximately four million to about 4.4 million Armenians, while the calculations of the Armenia Diaspora Conference, which is hosted by the Armenian Foreign Ministry, appear to be less conservative estimating the Armenian population outside Armenia at 11,267,304 (Tölölyan 2000: 107; Armenia Diaspora Conference n. y.). The Armenians and their communities are said to be spread over 80 to 102 countries (Avagian 1994: 75; Hofmann 1997b: 165). Here I will only give the figures on selected diaspora communities to give a brief overview.

Currently the largest diaspora communities are located in Russia and Georgia – the so-called "Inner Diaspora", which once was located in the domain of the

---

[6] According to statistics of the World Bank, in 2000 about 51% of Armenian emigrants have had more than 12 years of formal education, about 40% had attended school nine to twelve years and only 9% less than nine years (Adams 2003, cit. by Roberts&Banaian 2004: 36).

Soviet Union – as well as in the United States, France, and the countries in the Middle East, Lebanon, Iran and Syria, which, respectively, constitute the "Outer Diaspora" (Hofmann 1993: 79). The most influential, active and prosperous diaspora communities worldwide are supposed to be located in the United States and Canada (Lang&Walker 1991b: 49). The size of the Armenian diaspora in the United States is about 800,000 (Tölölyan 2000: 107). Los Angeles thereby hosts the biggest Armenian community in the Outer Diaspora with about 400,000 (Ishkanian 2002: 387; Redgate 1998: 275).

With about 2.5 million Armenians the diaspora in Russia has grown enormously in the last 15 years and, according to Hofmann, is contesting the diaspora's lead (Hofmann 2005: 17). However, Oussatcheva says that in terms of the political, organizational and financial potential the diaspora in Russia is not well-developed yet (Oussatcheva 2001: 10). In Europe, the Armenian diaspora in France with a size of 250,000 can be considered the most active and powerful (Aghanian 2007: 92-93; Tölölyan 2000: 107). Important centres for immigration are especially Paris, Lyon, and Marseille (Redgate 1998: 275). The countries in the Middle East - especially Lebanon, Syria and Iran - host historical Armenian settlements, which had been enlarged immensely by the post-genocidal migration (Dekmejian 1997: 424). In the last 30 to 40 years, though, the Armenian population in this region has shrunk considerably due to political unrest: 70,000 Armenians were estimated for Syria, 105,000 for Lebanon, with a concentration in Beirut, and 180,000 for Iran with Teheran, Tabriz, and Isfahan as main centres of the Armenian population (Tölölyan 2000: 107; Dekmejian 1997: 426).[7]

Further large communities, which were considerably diminished in the last century, are the Armenian communities in Nagorno-Karabakh/ Arzach (Azerbaijan) and in Turkey. Before the Nagorno-Karabakh conflict, another sizeable community of about 390,500 Armenians was situated in Azerbaijan. Meanwhile, 350,000 Armenians immigrated to Russia (Polm&Tauber 1997: 28; Hofmann 1997b: 167).

---

[7] Pre-migration figures were not mentioned in these sources.

After the eradication and flight of most Armenians during the genocide Turkey hosts about 60,000 Armenians; its main community is located in Istanbul (Tölölyan 2000: 107; Hofmann 1997b: 171-172).

3 Methods of field research and evaluation

In order to make my research transparent and comprehensible to the reader I will shortly depict how I collected my data. My research design was mainly interview-based. Apart from informal interviews, I used semi-structured interviews in order to explore the field and the question concerning cognitions on success. During the interviews I also focused on presumable "expert knowledge" of my informants. In this context, "expert knowledge" is defined as knowledge, which is not commonly shared, but which is due to a person's individual access, belonging or knowledge of a certain domain in a culture (see Bernard 2002: 182). The interviews contained questions about economic strategies, urban settling of the Armenian community, the establishment of institutions etc. I also conducted biographical interviews with selected interviewees, concentrating on the history of their migration and professional development. As examples of cultural practice these concrete life stories served for the further detection of immanent notions and strategies of success as well as for the crosscheck of the normative model of success, which was generated in the other interviews. This data was complemented by the generation of free lists of prominent Armenians who were supposed to embody "success stories".

Additionally, I drew information from "being there". Typically, participant observation shows to be difficult in the urban context as opportunities to take part in the informants' daily life are rather limited (Kokot 2007a: 19). This was also the case during my fieldwork as my access was mainly bound to public locations. Participant observation was therefore conducted on several events of the cultural association *Armenische Kulturverein zu Hamburg e.V.* (Armenian cultural association of Hamburg; further abbreviated: Kulturverein) and the youth organization *Armenischer Jugendverband Kilikia e.V.* (Armenian youth association Kilikia; abbreviation: Kilikia). Furthermore, I attended events like the Christmas mass in the church, the commemoration of the genocide on 24th April, a boxing match etc.

Many events and internal conversations (e.g. in the cultural association) were held in Armenian. Due to my lack of language knowledge, it was not possible for me to follow all events. The documentation of these events was limited mostly to the observable actions and their explanations or translations by Armenians. Moreover, I gained information via informal talks as well as from sources such as internet forums, websites, pamphlets and advertisements.

In total, I interviewed a dozen Armenians, among them more males than females. The gender imbalance thereby might be due to the concentration on (economically) successful individuals and to the way of sampling. In several cases the opportunity for interviews was limited to a single meeting. Still, a handful of persons served as key informants with whom I led multiple interviews and who could give information on different issues. None of my respondents had been born in Germany, but most of them had lived there for a significant length of time. The absolute duration of stay ranged between six and 30 years. Thus, all of my informants belonged to the first or second generation of Armenian immigrants.[1] Countries of origin comprised diverse countries in the Middle East as well as Armenia and other ex-Soviet countries. It has to be noted that the individuals of my sample shared certain characteristics: They were all living under rather secure conditions regarding the matter of legal residence; only in some cases the permit of residence was restricted to a certain period of time and bound to the purpose of studying or the working contract. Still, all of them were able to move freely and to work or follow their education. Almost all of them were in possession of an academic degree or they were pursuing one. A part of my informants were members of communal institutions; some of those were involved in community activities or projects to a certain extent. In those cases without membership it had been either cancelled or there had been no time or chance for the person to get involved in the community life. All of my interviewees were aware of the existence of Armenian community institutions in Hamburg and at least somehow felt to belong to

[1] With the term "First generation" I refer to those migrants who have experienced the act of immigration themselves. The "Second generation" consequently encompasses the descendants of this first generation who were born in the host country (see Wippermann&Flaig 2009: 3).

the diaspora – even if they did not belong to or visited one of the communal institutions. I also included talks with Armenians who actually did not live in Hamburg.

As the small size of the sample suggests my material cannot be used for quantitative analysis regarding the questions posed. Moreover, the amount of data on the diverse issues varies in size as it was not possible (or it was just not sensible in some cases) to ask all my informants the same questions. Therefore the evaluation oscillates between descriptive and analytical approaches to the material depending on the depth and thickness of the existent data. In its course, my findings will be compared to findings of other researches, whenever similarities in the research matters allow it. Furthermore, I will offer numerous direct quotations by my informants. In this way I want to give an insight into the data basis of my analysis and make my conclusions comprehensible and criticizable for the reader. As most interviews were held in German, most quotations have been translated into English. With respect to the small size of the community and the privacy of the informants involved, I will not only make the data anonymous but I will also refrain from giving more information on the quotation sources than needed. That means that sex, profession, age etc. will not be mentioned, as long as it does not compromise the quality of the analysis. Additionally, quotations may be altered slightly without manipulating the content, to avoid recognition of informants.

3.1 Reflections on the reality in the field and circumstances of research

At the beginning of the project, I was fortunate enough that a young Armenian woman contacted our institute for support as she was planning to write a paper on the Armenian Diaspora in Hamburg. She herself had been raised in a rather non-Armenian environment in Hamburg. Therefore, she also lacked any profound contact to the Armenian community and was in the position of a marginal observer. Her and I teamed up and started to visit events of the Armenian cultural association together.

Despite the warm welcoming I received as a researcher in the community I felt that latent insecurities existed in some of the conversations. Sometimes I had the impression that the recent integration discourse in the German public, which demanded the unequivocal declaration of non-Germans to a canon of liberal "western" values that were ascribed to German culture and society made some respondents defensive and eager to prove that the Armenians were not a segregative minority. Sometimes it seemed that interviewees were afraid that the Armenian community might be solely associated with the asylum seekers from Armenia, who were living under precarious conditions and thus – so it was conveyed to me – threatened the good reputation of the community. In such situations, I got aware of the fact that I represented the neighbouring "Other", a member of the majority culture. That fact also implied an uneven power relation, which might have had an impact on the interviews.

Another factor for cautiousness might have been the striving for the recognition of the genocide. According to Dabag the muteness of the Armenian diaspora in Germany for the last decades was substantially grounded in the presence of the large Turkish migrant community in Germany and the lack of Armenian political traditions in Germany (Dabag 1994: 11). Also my informants perceived the Turks as well-established, politically potent and numerically huge. Moreover, Germany, which had played an inglorious role as ally of the Ottoman Empire during the genocide, was perceived as a historical advocate of the Turkish side. In the past decades Armenian identity politics and cultural expression had been of rather low volume: Even the commemoration of the genocide on 24th April had only been hesitantly organized as a public event in the 1990s (Dabag 1994: 11). Recently, the tables seem to have turned a little as several events had taken place: The two Armenian umbrella organizations in Germany, the *Zentralrat der Armenier in Deutschland* (Central Council of Armenians in Germany) and the Diocese of the Armenian Apostolic Church in Germany, established the *Group of 24th April* which annually organizes the commemoration of the Armenian genocide as a public event in the Paulskirche in Frankfurt am Main – this event is usually supported by several German intellectuals who act as speakers and is covered by the German press. A further sign of Armenian agency was the erection of several stone crosses – a genuine Armenian cultural artifact (see 5.3) - in the German public in consensus with German municipalities. Also, several Armenian communities started – as will be discussed later – projects in order to buy or build churches of their own. Among them the Armenian association *Armenische Kirchen- und Kulturgemeinde Berlin e.V.* (Armenian religious and cultural association of Berlin), which asked their fellow countrymen to donate for the purchase of a church with the words: "It is time for us Armenians to set a landmark in the capital city of Germany" (Armenische Kirchen- und Kulturgemeinde Berlin e.V. 28.11.2006; translation by C.T.). In 2005, on the initiative of CDU/CSU[2], all fractions of the German Bundestag passed a resolution, which recognized the "deportations and massacres" of the Armenians during the events of 1915/16 and urged the German government to support Turkey's revision of its "historical guilt"[3]; moreover, the inclusion of the Armenian genocide into the curriculum of secondary schools was debated in the past years[4]. Finally, one might remember the openly shown indignation and grief of Armenians and non-Armenians over the presumably political murder of Hrant Dink[5], a journalist of Armenian ethnicity in Turkey, in January 2007. These events and actions give reason to believe in the rising of a new (political) self-consciousness of the Armenian diaspora in Germany. This development presented many chances but also risks for the Armenian community. Gains

---

[2] CDU and its Bavarian sister party CSU are the Christian Democratic Party and the Christian Social Union respectively. Both parties belong to the conservative party spectrum in Germany.

[3] Though the resolution did not categorize the massacres as genocide – a decision which was certainly anticipated by the Armenian side - the Turkish government condemned this move of the German Parliament harshly (Gesellschaft für bedrohte Völker 20.04.2005; netzeitung.de 16.06.2005; Evangelische Kirche in Deutschland 16.06.2005).

[4] After the inclusion of the genocide into German schoolbooks in Brandenburg in 2004 - the educational material had been produced by Mihran Dabag, a professor of Turkish Armenian origin teaching at the Institute of Research on Diaspora and Genocide of the University of Bochum – Turkey made use of its diplomatic weight to intervene and achieved the withdrawal of the curriculum change. Finally, on the critique by the Armenian ambassador, the latter decision was revised. For a documentation of the conflict see FAZ.NET 25.01.2007; Mönch 25.01.2005: 33; ibid. 27.01.2005: 35; ibid. 11.02.2005: 35; ibid. 21.07.2005: 31; Akyol 23.01.2006.

[5] Hrant Dink was an ethnic Armenian journalist in Turkey who spoke out for reconciliation between Armenians and Turks and was murdered on the streets of Istanbul in 2007. Even in Turkey thousands of Armenians and Turks took to the streets to show their dolour and indignation.

in the public sphere were confronted with harsh reactions from the Turkish side. The caution that I experienced during my research can also be interpreted in this context.

For this reason, it was not always easy to judge which kind of information I got was bearing a risk I was not aware of. Facts that seemed trivial or were publicly accessible sometimes were not easily discussed with some of my informants. For example, I had the impression that the building of the church and the aspects connected with it like donations, were not easily spoken about by all my informants. Meanwhile, information on that topic (such as the amount of donations) was freely available on the web site of the main Armenian association in Hamburg. I ascribe this paradox to the special situation of studying groups in one's own locality, where the generation of data, its evaluation and interpretation and thus, its manifestation, happen in the same place. Informants - as much as the researcher - thus cannot escape the (potential) impact of the "written culture" on their lives. While writing I took this responsibility into account and hope that I met its demands.

Another difficulty was connected to the character of the fieldwork as a "studying-up" research. Most of my interviewees were not "marginalized or powerless" individuals, which are usually in the focus of ethnographic or cultural studies (Gray 2007: 51). Rather they were actively and successfully participating in the economic realm and were in possession of higher education. This caused practical problems of access, mainly in the form of lack of time and space for encounters and made it difficult to conduct participant observation. Therefore, my data is rather to be perceived as representing discourses and norms than concrete cultural practice.

4 Armenian immigration and community building in Germany

In her research on the Armenian community in Manchester Aghanian maintains that the Armenians

> "[...] have a low visibility, receive little notice in the media and are neglected by the politicians, academics, social agencies that generally attend to migrant communities." (Aghanian 2007: 3)

Also Bakalian refers to the Armenians in the USA as a "hidden minority", which was until then left out by scientific research (Bakalian 1994: IX). These statements about relative inconspicuousness and little public attention can also be maintained for the Armenians in Germany (Ordukhanyan 2005: 221; Dabag 1995: 68). While other immigrant groups like the Turks are intensely covered by the media, the existence of Armenians in Germany is almost unknown to the broader German public.

Moreover, the establishment of an Armenian diaspora in Germany is a rather recent phenomenon (Meyer&Berkian 1988; Dabag 1995: 70). In contrast to other countries of residence like the USA, France, Syria and Lebanon, the main trigger for Armenian immigration to Germany was not the genocidal massacres in 1915/16 in the Ottoman Empire. On the contrary: Germany was avoided as it was an imperturbable ally of the Ottoman Empire during the First World War and later Turkey, and served as a destination of large-scale Turkish immigration in the 20th century. Thus, immigrating Armenians usually did not perceive Germany as a final destination, but as a transit country (Hofmann 1997a: 41). This attitude changed only recently with the arrival of the migrants from the Republic of Armenia after the collapse of the Soviet Union: They settled in Germany with a long-term perspective from the start (Tauber 1999: 29).

However, the first Armenian-German relations date back to the first crusade in 1097 and were further maintained primarily by trade (Dabag 1995: 66). Early Armenian settlements may also have existed as Mooradian mentions the founding of an Armenian printing office in 1680 in Leipzig (Mooradian 1970: 6). Nevertheless, significant immigration of Armenians to the German Empire began only at the end of the 19th century. In particular, Armenian students sojourned or immigrated for educational reasons, for example, from the Tsarist Empire to German University cities (Meyer 1988: 47; Dabag 1995: 66; see also Hofmann 1997a: 42-43).

The first stable diaspora communities developed at the turn of the 19th/20th century in the cities of Berlin, Leipzig, Dresden and Hamburg. Apart from students, it was merchants, industrials and refugees who then immigrated from the Tsarist and the Ottoman Empires (Hofmann 1997a: 43). In the aftermath of the genocide, as was mentioned above, few Armenians immigrated to Germany; if they did, their main destinations were the cities of Berlin and Hamburg (Dabag 1995: 67). Due to World War II Armenians entered Germany as prisoners of war or forced labourers from the invaded countries (Soviet Union, France, Greece and other European countries) as well as refugees from the Northern Caucasus, the Crimea and Russia, who dreaded Soviet repression after the withdrawal of German troops. Together with the exiled Armenians who had been employed in Germany during wartime they constituted the Displaced Persons (DPs) who were concentrated in Southern Germany from 1945 to 1955; most of them migrated further to the United States in the 1950s (Ordukhanyan 2005: 219, 222f.; Dabag 1995: 67).

With the implementation of the recruitment agreement between Germany and Turkey during the 1960s until 1973, approximately 13,000 Armenians came as guest workers from Turkey. After the Islamic Revolution in Iran, 5,000 Armenians fled to Germany to escape the discrimination against the Christian minority. A further 2,000 Armenians sought asylum from Arab countries, especially Lebanon and Syria, due to the political unrest (Polm&Tauber 1997: 29).[1] Many of these immigrants pursued naturalisation as soon as it was legally possible (Dabag 1995: 69).

Since 1991 Armenians from the Republic of Armenia first and foremost immigrated as asylum seekers. In the following subchapter, I will turn to further characteristics of this wave of migration on the basis of recent statistics.

Demographic and socio-economic data

As registration is based on nationality and not on ethnic or religious affiliation, statistics of German official authorities do not reveal complete figures on the Armenian diaspora in Germany. That means that, for example, ethnic Armenians of diasporic origin do not appear in the statistics. In the following I will offer first and foremost figures concerning those Armenian immigrants who are registered as such: The documented Armenians from the Republic of Armenia.

Still, estimations concerning the total number of Armenians in Germany exist. In 1998, the Diocese of the Armenian Apostolic Church estimated the number of ethnic Armenians at 30,000 to 35,000 (Diözese der Armenischen Kirche in Deutschland 1998: 20). According to the official statistics on the Armenians from the Republic of Armenia numbers are such: In 1999, more than 11,000 Republic Armenians[2] lived in Germany (Statistisches Bundesamt 2007a: 20). Thus, the latter may have accounted for approximately a third of the total Armenian population at these times. Three years later post-Soviet immigration reached its peak when 11,442 Armenians from the Republic dwelled in Germany; after this year the figure fell slightly but steadily to approximately 10,000 Armenians in 2006 (Statis-

[1] It must be assumed that these figures by Tauber and Polm are estimates as there are no precise statistics available.

[2] I have formed the artificial expression "Republic Armenian" for those Armenians whose origin is the Republic of Armenia. This term might not be very elegant, but it helps as the differentiation along geographical origin plays an eminent role in the Armenian diaspora.

tisches Bundesamt 2007a: 25). This decrease was partly due to naturalisation (see figure 1).

It appears that the annual quota of naturalisation acts has more than tripled in the years from 1999 to 2006 (Statistisches Bundesamt 2007b: 19-20, 22-23). This increase of naturalisation acts may be due to the fact that, by now, more and more immigrants reside for eight or more years in Germany and, thus, may apply for naturalisation.[3]

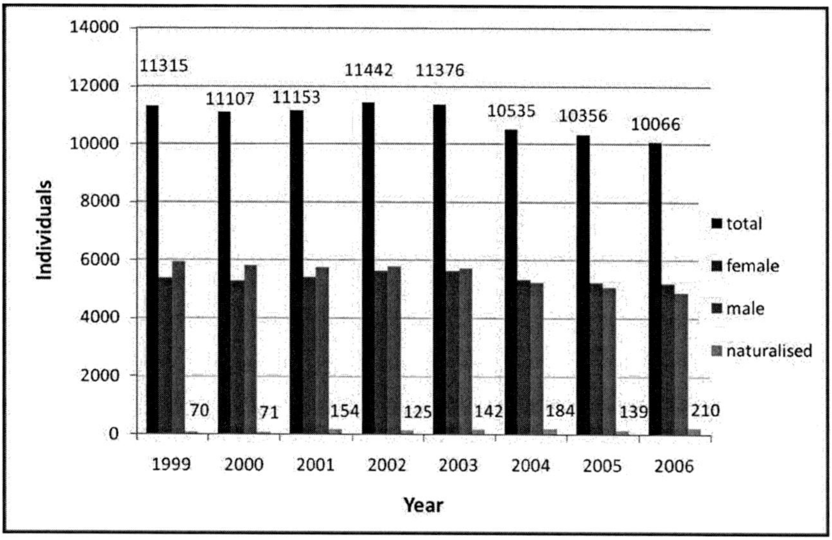

figure 1 Republic Armenian population in Germany according to sex and acts of naturalisation (1999-2006). Source of data: Statistisches Bundesamt 2007a: 20-25; ibid. 2007b: 18-19, 22-2.

Though, as mentioned above, the official number of Armenians from the Republic has decreased in the last years, one of my informants stated that the total number of Armenians has probably increased by about 20,000 in the past

[3] In 2006 this applied to almost half of the immigrants from the Republic of Armenia (Statistisches Bundesamt 2007a: 52, 54).

decade. This figure may either be valued as over-estimation or as taking into account an on-going migration from the Armenian diaspora and/ or unknown and possibly high number of undocumented migrants.

One important strategy of immigration from Armenia has been the request of asylum: In 1996, Armenians from the Republic constituted the seventh biggest group of asylum seekers in Germany (approx. 3,510 requests). The number of requests steadily decreased by approximately 65% in the following five years – thereby it followed the general trend of decline[4] (Bundesamt für Migration und Flüchtlinge 2006: 28, 31; Hofmann 2005: 76). The vast majority of Republic Armenians is yet to be recognised as legal and/ or permanent residents: In 2004 more than three quarter were living under the conditions of suspended deportation (Ger.: *Duldung*[5]); in contrast, about 13% were in possession of an unlimited residence permit (Ger.: *unbefristete Aufenthaltsgenehmigung*) (Statistisches Bundesamt 2006: 68-69). In 2006 the number of those living under suspended deportation had decreased to less than a third of this value (Statistisches Bundesamt 1997a: 77). Furthermore, 5% had a permission to reside temporarily for the length of the asylum procedure and one in ten had no legal status at all – thus, about 42% lived under precarious legal conditions (Statistisches Bundesamt 2007a: 77). In 2006 it was still a minority of about 18%, who were in possession of an unlimited permit of residence (Statistisches Bundesamt 2007a: 77-78). Meanwhile, the recognition of asylum is hardly granted: In 2001 six requests were granted, while 263 deportations were executed (Hofmann 2005: 76). Therefore,

---

[4] The total number of requests for asylum decreased between 1993 and 2005 from about 320,000 to 28,914. This was due to stricter German asylum policy, which was enforced by the reform of article 16a of the German Constitution, including the "Third Country Regulation" (Ger.: *Drittstaatenregelung*) and the principle of "safe country of origin" (Ger.: *sicheres Herkunftsland*). (Bundesamt für Migration und Flüchtlinge 2006: 23; Bade&Oltmer 2004: 112, 114).

[5] The status "suspended deportation" is not a legal title of residence, but entitles the asylum seeker to residence for a defined time period during which deportation is suspended (Bade&Oltmer 2004: 79). This status is connected with restriction in movement and employment. Also, since 1993 newly arrived asylum seekers are distributed among the federal states according to a specific allocation formula rendering voluntary choice of the place of residence impossible (Bundesamt für Migration und Flüchtlinge 2007: 11-12).

most of the recent immigrants in Germany are still threatened by deportation or the expiration of their limited residence permit.

The spatial distribution of the diaspora in Germany can be reconstructed by a map of Armenian organizations (see map 1). It suggests that the largest settlements of the first waves of migration from the Middle Eastern countries are, with the exception of Berlin and Hamburg, mainly located in the southern and western regions of Germany (Bavaria, Baden-Württemberg, Hesse, North-Rhine-Westphalia and Lower Saxony). Urban centres of settlement are Cologne, Stuttgart, Munich, Berlin, Frankfurt a.M., the Ruhr area, as well as Hannover and Hamburg. Also the location of more recent migrants from the Republic of Armenia does not deviate a lot from this spatial distribution as most of them are registered in North-Rhine-Westphalia, Hesse, Lower Saxony and Bavaria. A considerable number of Armenians also live in the East of Germany, namely Mecklenburg-Western Pomerania (see figure 2).

map 1 Spatial distribution of Armenian organizations in Germany. By Caroline Thon.

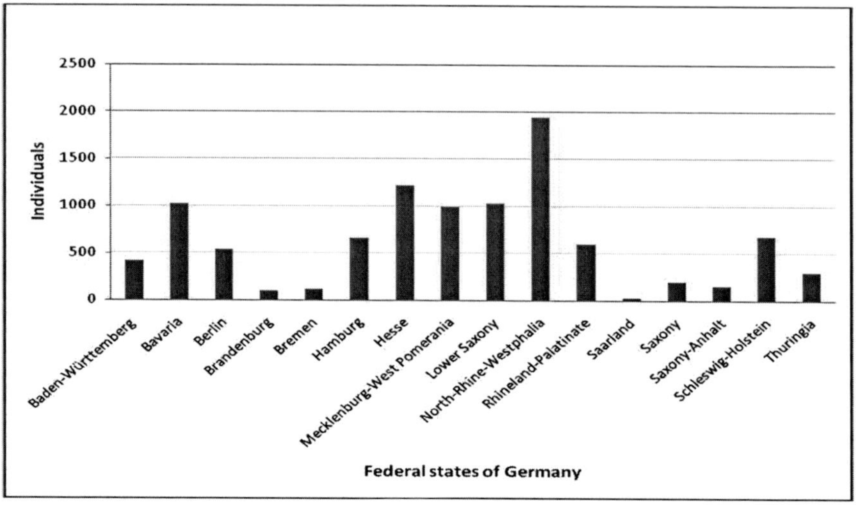

figure 2 Republic Armenian population in Germany according to distribution to federal states (31.12.2006). Source of data: Statistisches Bundesamt 2007a: 58-59.

Still, these figures oppose Tauber's assumption that Mecklenburg-Western Pomerania in East Germany – being a preferred destination for the accommodation of asylum seekers by the German authorities and, at the same time, being cut off from the centres of Armenian settlements – is the main location of Republic Armenians (Tauber 1999: 43). However, related to the total population, Mecklenburg-Western Pomerania (approx. 0.06%) has the highest density of Republic Armenians, closely followed by Hamburg, Schleswig-Holstein, Hesse and Bremen; the average density in Germany being about 0.016% (calculations by C.T. based on data of Statistisches Bundesamt 2007a: 59 and Statistische Ämter des Bundes und der Länder 29.01.2008).

Statistical socio-economic data on the Armenians in Germany is not available. According to Dabag, in the 1960s the Armenian migrants' community mainly comprised doctors, merchants and students (Dabag 1995: 67). With the immigration of Turkish Armenians under the guest worker contract, mostly workers, small retailers and manual workers came to Germany. Armenians from the subsequent immigration waves from Iran and the Arab countries were primarily merchants or craftsmen (Dabag 1995: 67). Data on the socio-economic situation of recent migrants from Armenia is also not available. But it has to be assumed that their working situation is strongly influenced by their legal status. According to the current legislation, allowance of employment or self-employment is only granted to migrants who are entitled to permanent residence or whose permit was explicitly granted for employment reasons (Ger.: *Aufenthalt zum Zwecke der Beschäftigung*). This applied to almost 2,000 Armenian migrants in 2006, i.e. 19% of the total (Statistisches Bundesamt 2007a: 76-77). Allowance of employment of all other residence permit status groups can only be gained by special permission by the German Federal Employment Office (Aufenthaltsgesetz §4 Abs. 2 AufenthG; §9 Abs. 1 AufenthG).

Concerning the prevalence of self-employment Dabag states that due to the immigration wave by Armenians as guest workers from Turkey the Armenian diaspora in Germany was dominated by employees (about 95%). This contrasts with higher rates[6] of self-employment in the other diaspora communities. Nevertheless, self-employment is said to be increasing among the Armenians in Germany (Dabag 1995: 67).

Armenian institutions in Germany

The institutional landscape of the Armenian diaspora in Germany is young and still developing. The typical, internationally overarching and transnational diaspora institutions, namely the Church and the Diaspora parties, are either young or hardly visible. Also, the Armenian printing press, which, together with the Armenian Apostolic Church and the organizations of communal cultural life, belongs to the pillars of the Armenian diasporic structure, is hardly developed (Hofmann 1997a: 47). In contrast, the organizational life at the local and regional level is

[6] Dabag does not mention any concrete figures here.

well established. Regarding the spatial distribution of institutions, the main centres of Armenian institutional life are in the western and southern regions of Germany (see map 1). The first Armenian community, *Verein der armenischen Kolonie zu Berlin*, was established in Berlin in 1923. It came to an end during the Second World War (Hofmann 1997a: 44). After 1945 Armenians who lived as Displaced Persons in Esslingen, Stuttgart, built a further Armenian community (Ordukhanyan 2005: 232). This community enjoyed a rich social, cultural and economic life and – though it was eventually diminished due to emigration in the end of the 1940s - contributed to the cultural activity and the establishment of the later organizations, which have been built by the Armenian immigrants since the 1960s and 1970s (Ordukhanyan 2005: 224f.).

This process of establishment of the basic communal structure of the Armenian diaspora, namely secular cultural associations (Ger.: *Kulturverein*) and religious associations (Ger.: *Kirchengemeinde*, *Kirchenverein*)[7], of which the latter are bound to the Armenian Church, is still going on (Dabag 1995: 70). In 1993 Hofmann mentioned 20 organizations, while Tauber counted 33 local and regional organizations at the end of the 1990s (Hofmann 1997a: 46; Tauber 1999: 44). In 2008 about 40 Armenian organizations could be found, which could be classified as either *Kulturverein* or *Kirchengemeinde* Hofmann maintains that their communal roles are similar as both institutional types chiefly provide the maintenance of Armenian traditions, Armenian language courses, celebrations of Armenian holidays and information about Armenian culture to the German public. Due to the pattern of settlement of the Armenians in the 1960s and 1970s, community structures were first built up in the industrial hot-spots of Germany (Hofmann 1997a: 46).

Further Armenian organizations in Germany comprise a women's association, several sports clubs, artist associations as well as philanthropic organizations,

---

[7] According to Hofmann the founding of a "Kirchenverein" or "Gemeinde" was common in communities that were dominated by Turkish Armenians (Hofmann 1997a: 46).

which are, for example, concerned with the support of Armenia, the Armenian cultural heritage or the needs of Armenian migrants from Armenia. Furthermore, a handful of students' clubs or youth organizations exist on this level. From the 1970s to the mid-1990s six Armenian academic and research institutes were opened, of which two are incorporated into German universities. Briefly, issues of these institutions are the documentation and research on Armenian culture and history as well as research on the Armenian genocide.

Besides, the *Deutsch-Armenische Gesellschaft* - DAG (German Armenian Society) has to be mentioned as a historically important institution for Armenian life in Germany. It was founded on the initiative of the Dashnak party in 1914 by several Armenians from diverse countries in cooperation with several German personalities of clerical and academic background, among them Dr Johannes Lepsius who acted as the first chairman and Dr Paul Rohrbach, his vice-chairman (Hofmann 1997a: 43). In its history, the DAG often acted as political advocate of the Armenians in Germany, but was also politically involved as mediator between the Armenians in the Ottoman Empire and the German government. By its lobbying it also averted the classification of Armenians as Semites by the race policy during the period of German National Socialism (Hofmann 2005: 70). Several German intellectuals and artists (e.g. Thomas Mann, Georg Simmel, Max Liebermann) were members of the DAG (Dabag 1995: 71). The DAG also publishes the quarterly *Armenisch-Deutsche Korrespondenz*, which is one of two existent publications; the other one is *Karun*, a tri-lingual monthly (Turkish, Armenian, German), which is published in Bruchsal. Generally, the establishment of publications in the Armenian language is complicated by the fact that a large part of the Armenian diaspora in Germany is not in command of their "mother tongue": About 60 to 80% of the Turkish Armenians in Germany are not proficient in Armenian as the repressive education and minority policies in Turkey have impeded the learning of the language (Hofmann 1997a: 47). Therefore, attempts to establish Armenian-language publications were often short-lived (Hofmann 1997a: 47).

The institutional integration of the Armenian organizations is served by two umbrella organizations: The central union of Armenians in Germany, *Zentralrat der Armenier in Deutschland* (ZAD), and the Diocese of the Armenian Apostolic Church in Cologne, *Armenisch-Apostolische Diözese zu Köln*. The history of the ZAD reaches back to 1969. Only a minority of Armenian organizations in Germany is organized in the ZAD: In 1993, it was twelve of the then-existing Armenian associations (Hofmann 1997a: 46), while it was 11 organizations in 2008[8]. In between, the number of member organizations had shrunk to six in 1998 (Tauber 1999: 47). The tasks of the ZAD are located on different levels of diasporic work: Promotion and coordination of cultural and charitable activities; promotion of youth with regard to identity and integration; cultural exchange and cooperation with German institutions; transnational cooperation with Armenian institutions in Armenia, the EU and other countries; establishment of a network among Armenian organizations in Germany (see Zentralrat der Armenier in Deutschland n.y. b). Its sub-organization *Junge Armenier* (Young Armenians) organizes the "Jugendtreff" twice a year, an event, where Armenian youth from the whole Germany meet for several days for cultural and leisure activities. The sub-organization *Armenisches Sportkommittee* (Armenian sports committee) organizes the German Armenian participants of the Pan-Armenian Games.

The Diocese of the Armenian Apostolic Church was founded in 1992. It belongs to the Catholicosate of Etschmiadzyn (Hofmann 1997b: 182). The clergy consists of the Primate Archbishop Karekin Bekdjian in Cologne, two archimandrites in Cologne and Erlangen, one priest in Hanau and eleven deacons in different cities and towns. In 1998, a former Catholic church in Cologne was transformed into an Armenian Apostolic church called *Surb Sahak-Mesrop*. Nine of the religious community organizations in Germany are organized under the umbrella of the Diocese[9]. In comparison to the cultural associations, which are founded on independent statutes, the members of the Diocese are united under the organization's

[8] For member organizations of the ZAD see: Zentralrat der Armenier in Deutschland n.y. b.
[9] For member organizations see Armenien.de 12.04.2007.

statutes. Nonetheless, several cultural associations have the special permission from the Diocese to offer regular service in churches. This is possible as the ecumenical cooperation with the German Catholic and Protestant churches allows the holding of the services in the latter's church buildings (Hofmann 1997a: 47). Currently at least two projects exist, which aim at the construction of a genuine Armenian church: The communities of the Rhine/Main area, which had announced their project officially in January 2008 had collected about 12,000€ in July 2008 for a church building in Hanau[10]; the community of Hamburg had also launched a call for donations for a church of its own in July 2007. Besides those projects, the *Armenische Kirchen- und Kulturgemeinde Berlin e.V.*, an Armenian community organization in Berlin, appealed to the Armenians to support the purchase of a church building (Armenische Kirchen- und Kulturgemeinde Berlin e.V. 28.11.2006).

Already Tauber noted that the Diocese and the ZAD collide in their respective aspirations and self-perception as the one institution which sustains the overarching structure of the Armenian communities in Germany and coordinates the social and cultural life in the diaspora – a fact that had also raised conflict in the past (Diözese der Armenischen Kirche in Deutschland 1998: 20-21; Tauber 1999: 47). Nonetheless, both organizations work together in the *Gruppe 24. April* (Group of April 24th), which organizes the main event on the commemoration day of the genocide in the Paulskirche in Frankfurt a.M.

Apart from the Church, which had been *the* transnational Armenian institution from early times on, other classical, transnationally operating organizations, namely the Diaspora parties and their respective affiliate social institutions, are hardly visible or just emerging. This contrasts with other Armenian communities - for example Thessalonica, Athens (see Schwalgin 2004: 95f.), Aleppo etc. - where the existence and agency of Diaspora parties is an essential part of community life. However, there are traces of involvement of the Dashnakzutyun and,

[10] See the website of the Rhein-Main-communities: Armenier in RheinMain 2008.

recently, also of the Ramgavar party in Germany. According to an interviewee, there are two offices of the Dashnak in Germany (Munich and Dusseldorf). Moreover, the *Armenian Relief Society*[11] (ARS, or the Armenian abbreviation: HOM), a philanthropic organization, as well as *Nor Serunt* (New Generation), the youth branch of the Dashnak, have been established in Germany probably in the course of the last 10 years. This is peculiar as a glance at history shows that the diaspora in Germany has also been shaped by the Dashnak party. Hofmann mentions that a delegate of the central organ of the Dashnak party in Constantinople was entrusted with the establishment of an "Armenian-German Committee", which resulted in the founding of the Deutsch-Armenische Gesellschaft in Berlin in 1914 (Hofmann 1997a: 43). Another source confirms the opening of an office of the Dashnak in Berlin in the year 1922 (Petrosjan 1999 cit. by Tauber 1999: 44). Furthermore, in the 1940s a branch of the *Dashnak Armenian National Committee* existed in Stuttgart, which organized the dispersed Armenians in Hamburg, Munich, Frankfurt a.M., Bremen, Berlin and Osnabruck and maintained contact with non-Armenian institutions in post-war Germany. Further, the DPs' camp in Stuttgart was organized to a broad extent by the Dashnak party and its different organizations until its dissolution in 1949 (Ordukhanyan 2005: 225-230).

Furthermore, in May and June 2008 two Young Professional organizations of the *Armenian General Benevolent Union* (AGBU)[12] were opened in Cologne and Frankfurt a.M. The AGBU is generally associated with the Ramgavar Party (Bakalian 1994: 186). Another students' club called *HAIK* founded in 2003 in Mannheim, can also be classified as a Young Professional organization. It is also financially supported by the AGBU and its office in Frankfurt hosts one of the AGBU's newly-found organizations (see HAIK 2008).

---

[11] The Armenian Relief Society was founded in New York in 1910 as suborganization of the Dashnak party and assists welfare to the Armenian people (Lang&Walker 1991b: 50).

[12] The *Armenian General Benevolent Union* was founded in Cairo in 1906 and has its main seat in New York today. The transnational organization is active in cultural and educational work and is most renowned for its literary publication and the financial support of students (Aghanian 2007: 159).

Another transnationally operating philanthropic organization is the *"Hayastan" All-Armenian Fund,* which was set up in Dachau in 1993. The main body was founded in 1992 by the then-incumbent Armenian president Levon Ter-Petrossian in Yerevan. It comprises local committees in 17 countries and concerts the internationally spread financial aid for the rebuilding of the Republic of Armenia and Arzach. Under the umbrella of the fund – as it is proudly declared in the organization's brochure – rivalling groups such as the Diaspora parties and their respective benevolent organizations, come together in the foundation board ("Hayastan" All-Armenian Fund 05.11.2007).

5 Armenian migration to Hamburg and community building

Comparing the Armenian diaspora communities in Germany, Hamburg – together with Berlin and Leipzig – belongs to the eldest Armenian settlements. It was founded at the turn of the 19th century (Harutunian 2002/03). Tauber ascribes the attraction of Hamburg at these times to its character as a port city and metropolis of trade (Tauber 1999: 50). According to the information of an interviewee, in 1913 or 1914 a German-Armenian trade organization was founded in Hamburg, which enabled Armenians to expand their merchant activities to Northern Europe. The project was short-lived for the organization was closed down at the start of World War I. After the roots of the community were laid by a trade diaspora, several waves of migration followed in the 20th century. Migration patterns changed and the community in Hamburg lost its character as a trade diaspora[1] (Tauber 1999: 55). Though, this decline of commercial activity might be halted with a further consolidation of the diaspora: As one Armenian businessman let me know, he planned to establish an honorary consulate in Hamburg in order to facilitate and enhance business relations between Hamburg and Armenia.

The first Armenians who settled as merchants in Hamburg originated primarily from Tsarist Russia, the Ottoman Empire and the city of Tabriz in Persia. The number of Armenians in Hamburg before the Second World War was about 50 to 100[2] (Tauber 1999: 57). The Armenians from the Ottoman Empire and Tsarist Russia had also often emigrated for political reasons: The Russian Revolution and the genocide in the Ottoman Empire. Tauber states that at this time Armenians enjoyed a common social life, though an emic differentiation into subgroupings by geographical origin already existed (ibid. 1999: 58-59).

[1] Tauber mentions that nowadays only a minority was active in the import-export business (ibid. 1999: 50). This statement tallies with my information (see 5.2).

[2] Figure estimated by an informant of Tauber.

From 1950 up to the 1960s, Armenians from Lebanon, Syria and Persia immigrated for educational purposes to Hamburg. Difference in age and social backgrounds between the students and the merchants brought about that deeper contact to the well-established merchant families rarely existed (Tauber 1999: 59-60). During the 1960s, Armenian migration from Lebanon and Syria augmented (ibid.1999: 63). Immigration of Armenians from Turkey started after the German-Turkish recruitment agreement. In 1965, the Armenians from Syria, Lebanon and Persia who had immigrated in the 1950s founded the *Armenischer Kulturverein zu Hamburg e.V.* The established Armenian merchant families also attended the club (ibid. 1999: 60). During these times, Tauber reports, the organized community, which was still small, was perceived as "a big family" (ibid. 1999: 62; translation by C.T.) – a feeling that vanished in the following years. Further waves of immigration, of a greater scale, increased the heterogeneity regarding countries of origin, social status, educational level, age and length of residence in Germany (ibid. 1999: 62).

With the event of the Islamic Revolution in 1979, more Armenians immigrated as asylum seekers (Tauber 1999: 63). Until the 1990s, Germany was in general not appreciated as the final destination of migration. In particular, the Armenians who fled the Islamic Revolution in Iran were eager to migrate further to the USA[3] - the only exception were the Armenians from Turkey whose majority remained in Hamburg (ibid. 1999: 62). Thus, the Armenian migration pattern tended to be based on the idea of sojourning. This strong fluctuation of newcomers and emigrants formed the community in Hamburg and presented a problem to the establishment of solid organizational structures.

3 Asylum policy in times of the Islamic Revolution was thus that Armenians from Iran who planned to migrate to USA had to migrate first to a European country in order to apply for asylum. In Germany, Armenians who wanted to seek asylum in the USA had to apply for asylum in Germany at the same time. As a result, Armenians who were rejected by the USA still had the chance to receive asylum from Germany (Information by a respondent from Iran).

This pattern of migration dramatically changed with the arrival of the Armenians from the Republic of Armenia. They were the first Armenian immigrants who – from the start – chose Germany as their final destination of migration (Tauber 1999: 29). Republic Armenians primarily immigrated as asylum seekers, while a presumably small number came on the basis of working contracts or as students.[4] Meanwhile, especially Iranian Armenians continued to migrate further to the USA as they often had kin there.

As it was mentioned above, heterogeneity always accompanied the history of the community. Tauber mentioned the differentiation of Armenians according to their regional origin and dialect, viz. Western and Eastern Armenian. In this respect Turkey and the Middle Eastern host countries of post-genocide migration (Lebanon, Jordan, Syria etc.) belong to Western Armenian region and Armenia and Iran (of which the latter was mainly populated by deported migrants from the Eastern Armenian region in the 16th century) are part of the Eastern Armenian region. Furthermore, a refined sub-categorization with regard to the country or even city of origin existed. These differences accounted for certain internal conflicts and cleavages (Tauber 1999: 75f.).

The perception of these cultural differences was diminished when the Armenians from the Republic of Armenia arrived. According to the resident Armenians, who by now also referred to themselves as "Diaspora Armenians", the new immigrants not only displayed a different attitude or habitus (see 6.2), but also were said to socialize with Russian immigrants. This was mentioned particularly with regard to Armenian youth who were feared to join Russian youth gangs, and thus, distance themselves from the community and end up in delinquency. Despite this negative

---

[4] One phenomenon in Hamburg is the presence of several academics from the University of Yerevan due to its academic cooperation with the research centre for particle physics and electron acceleration, *Deutsches Elektronen-Synchrotron* (DESY) in Bahrenfeld. Since the 1990s, approximately 30 academics from Armenia have been employed there. Seven or eight families have settled there being employed on temporary working contracts, which were, though, extended in the recent years (according to respondents from the Armenian Republic).

association with the Russian legacy among Diaspora Armenians, it remained meaningful to some Republican Armenians I met.

Demographic and socio-economic data

Official numbers regarding the total number of ethnic Armenians in Hamburg are not available for the reason mentioned before in chapter 4. With regard to the total number of ethnic Armenians, estimations by Tauber's informants range between 2,000 and 4,000 individuals (Tauber 1999: 51). The proportions concerning national origin were estimated to be 50% Republic Armenians, 20% Iranian Armenians, 20% Turkish Armenians and 10% of Syrian and Lebanese Armenians (Tauber 1999: 52). Regarding the recent immigration from Armenia, about 700 Armenians from the Republic of Armenia were registered in 2007 in Hamburg. Similar to the total migration to Germany, migration to Hamburg had its peak in 2001 (772 individuals) and, thereafter, slightly decreased (see figure 3).

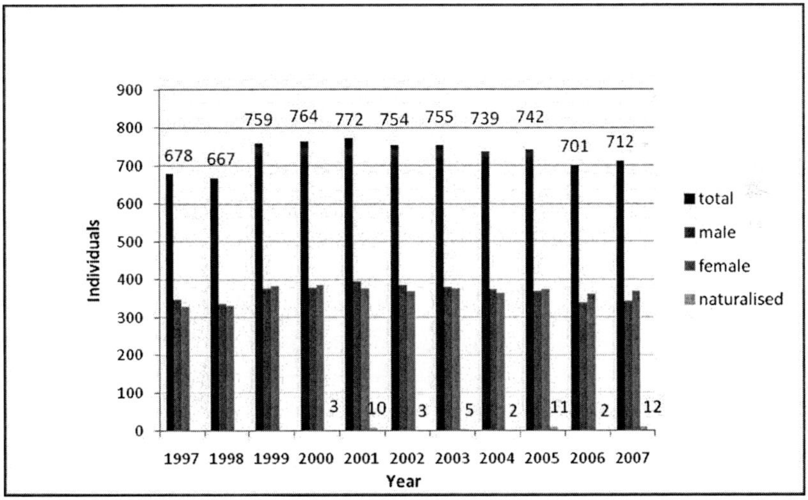

figure 3 Republic Armenian population in Hamburg according to sex and acts of naturalisation (1997-2007) [1] Source of data: Hamburger Melderegister n.y. b; Statistikamt Nord n.y..

As these figures show naturalization cannot be seen as a significant or stable factor yet; the quota of naturalized Armenians ranges between 0.3 and 1.7 in the years 2000 to 2007. With regard to immigration and emigration, also it shows that there is no stable tendency apart from a decrease in the absolute number of movements (see figure 4).

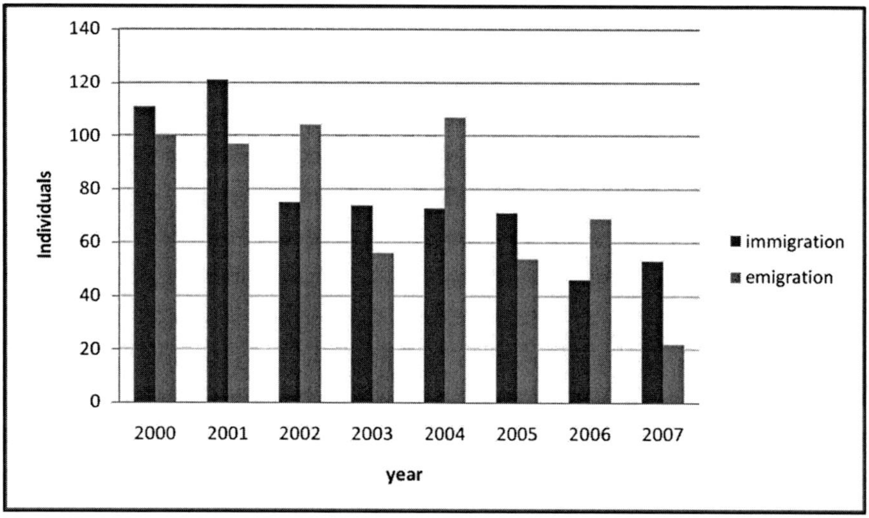

figure 4 Republic Armenian population in Hamburg according to immigration and emigration (2000-2007). Source of data: Statistikamt Nord n.y.

While the first merchant families who settled in Hamburg preferred dwellings in the quarters near the Alster, today a specific geographical distribution or significant concentration of ethnic Armenians in urban space cannot be asserted on the basis of the available data (see also Tauber 1999: 52, 58). According to official data of 2004, the distribution of registered Armenians from the Republic of Armenia in Hamburg proved to be as follows (see map 2): Roughly two-thirds lived in the districts of Wandsbek, Hamburg-Nord, and Altona. Quarters with a high density[5] of Republic Armenians were Lehmsahl-Mellingstedt, which is located on the northern rim of Hamburg, Sinstorf in the south, Curslack in the south east of Hamburg as well as Borgfelde and Hohenfelde, which are located close to the city centre. While the former three quarters are spatially separated almost to the maximum, Hohenfelde and Borgfelde neighbour each other on the eastern side of the Alster and adjoin Uhlenhorst, where the Armenian associations are located. Most quarters with a high absolute Republic Armenian population[6] are located in the outskirts, namely Langenhorn, Lehmsahl-Mellingstedt, Osdorf, Rahlstedt and Bergedorf; areas closer to the urban core – Hohenfelde, Borgfelde and Winterhude - tend to be east of the Alster. Bahrenfeld is an exception in this context. Regarding the socio-economic fabric, most of these quarters are average or above average[7].

While this data does not allow final conclusions about the distribution of Armenians over urban space, it shows at least that even though the Republic Armenians constitute a rather homogeneous group of immigrants regarding origin, cultural background, legal status, time of immigration, and context factors they did not build significant clusters in urban space. Also in other countries the decentralized settling of Armenians in their respective cities of residence was observed by several researchers and may be put down to heterogeneity of migration flows (Talai 1986: 251; Mesrobian 2000: 23). An exception to this "settlement pattern" is, for example, the former Armenian ghettos in Athens. These developed out of refugee camps set up by the Greek state and were mainly filled with Greek and Armenian fleeing the invasion of Smyrna (today: Izmir) by the Turks in 1922 (Schwalgin 2004: 63-66). In the case of Hamburg, the

[5] Density here means the percentage of Republic Armenians regarding the total population of a respective quarter. The average density of Republic Armenians in Hamburg was about 0.04% in 2004 (calculations by C.T. based on Hamburger Melderegister n. y. a; Statistikamt Nord 2005).
[6] Due to the low total number I will refer here to quarters with more than 20 Armenian/quarter.
[7] The data basis here is an analysis of the social structure and ranking of the 92 largest quarters of Hamburg relying on data of 2006. Parameters included, for example, rates of unemployment, welfare recipients, living space per person, quota of inhabitants without graduation. See Grüne Alternative Liste 17.01.2008.

data also shows that the immigrants mostly did not settle in socio-economically disadvantaged areas, but tend to prefer quarters that range between average and well off.

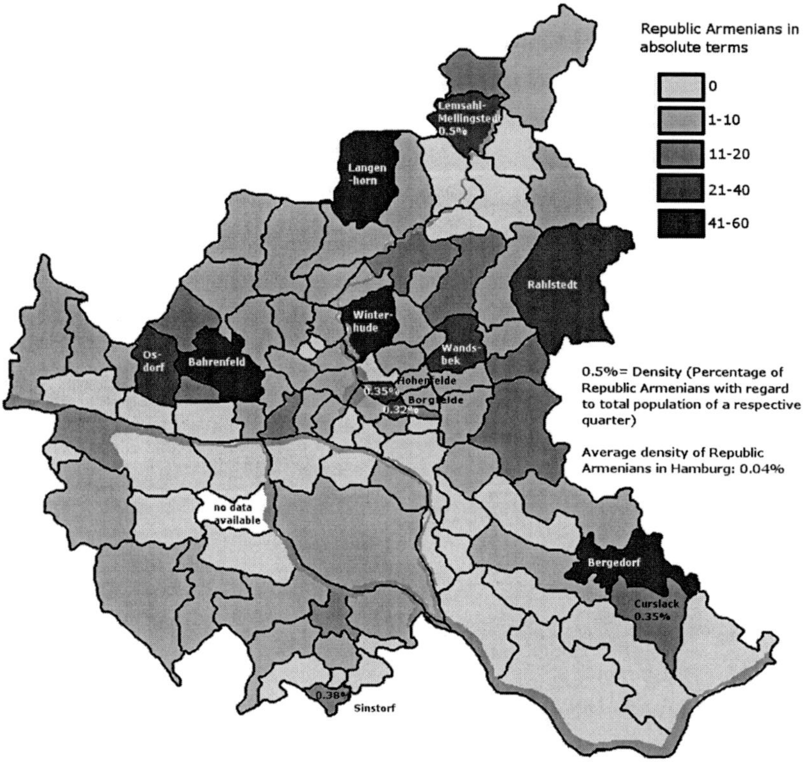

map 2 Spatial distribution of Republic Armenians in Hamburg in 2004. Source of data: Hamburger Melderegister n.y. a (data of 2004); Statistikamt Nord 2005 (data of 2004). By Caroline Thon.

5.1 Diaspora institutions and elites

Here I will introduce the obviously relevant, visibly manifested networks – the communal institutions. Referring to Tölölyan's concept of "diasporists/diaspora elites", I also investigated whether the Armenian diaspora community in Hamburg and also Germany was in possession of proactive diasporic forces and which positions they occupied in the diasporic landscape.

Institutions of the community in Hamburg

The organizational structure of the Armenian community in Hamburg is mainly shaped by the Armenian cultural association *Armenischer Kulturverein zu Hamburg e.V.*, which was founded in 1965. All further local associations emanated from this first association. Fragmentation of the community thus had resulted from secession processes; though, two of the following associations, viz. the Kulturverein and the Youth organization *Armenischer Jugendverband Kilikia e.V.* (founded in 2007), which were presumably the most active and accessible, still resided under the same roof and cooperate with each other. Tauber also mentioned the existence of a women's association, *Frauenverein*, which was organized as an informal meeting in 1983 and used the building of the Kulturverein. Moreover, in 1996 the *Kirchenverein* ("church association") was founded and officially registered in 1998 (Tauber 1999: 53).

Still, as Tauber recorded also during her fieldwork, only a small number of Armenians was organized in those associations and, thus, took an active part in community life (ibid. 1999: 52-53). The Kulturverein reached about 120 families[8] in 2007; Kilikia had about 40 official members in 2007. The number of members of the Kirchenverein was not available to me. During my research I did not encounter any member of the Kirchenverein, which resulted of a schism between members of the Kulturverein. According to Tauber, in 1998 it comprised about 20 to 22

[8] Tauber mentions that about 100 families were paying membership fees (ibid. 1999: 66).

members who were mainly Turkish Armenians who had not been in contact with the Kulturverein before as well as Armenians from Lebanon, Syria and Iran who had quit their active membership in the latter organization due to disagreements. According to its statutes, the Kirchenverein gathers every first Sunday in the church of St. Gertrud (ibid. 1999: 53-54). Among the members the Kulturverein the activities and the structure of the Kirchenverein seemed to be hardly known. Respondents who were not actively involved in the community life of the Kulturverein did not know about it at all. One respondent described the Kirchenverein and its activities as follows:

> "[...] I don't know any activities organized by this group, I don't know what they have done there, apart from the choir, whenever I went to church service - I didn't notice anything else. Well, when they gather, they make coffee parties, they natter. Okay, fair enough for them, that's nice. But as an association, as an active association - I have not perceived them like that. No events. Maybe I am little informed about that. But I think if they had done great work, I would have heard of it - at least indirectly - here in Hamburg."

As the Armenian Apostolic Diocese in Cologne and a priest from Berlin were responsible for all religious matters in the community (i.e. the arrangement of services), according to my informants, the Kirchenverein did not have any influential position in the community of Hamburg. Relations between the two organizations seemed to be reduced or even non-existent. According to the informant mentioned above, members of the Kirchenverein seldom attended events by the Kulturverein. Tauber also mentioned that the Kirchenverein broke off from the Diocese, when it created its own statutes instead of taking over the statutes of the latter (ibid. 1999: 54). It further remained unclear whether the informal Frauenverein still existed, which was said to use the building of the Kulturverein for its gatherings and which had around 15 members at the end of 1990 (ibid. 1999: 53) was not visible for me. Diaspora parties had not established themselves in the community of Hamburg – at least not visibly. I was told that party affiliations were rather handled as a private matter. The influence of party affiliation on (institutional) community life was rather feared as it could cause further fragmentation. In the following, I will only refer to the Kulturverein and Kilikia as the only associations that were visible and accessible for me.

As was mentioned above, the cultural association "Armenischer Kulturverein zu Hamburg e.V." was founded in 1965 and, at the time of my research, had approximately 120 registered members. It was located in the East of Hamburg (Uhlenhorst), and was open on Friday evenings and the whole of Saturday. It also offered a website since autumn 2007 (see Armenischer Kulturverein zu Hamburg e.V. n.y. a). Members were informed about upcoming events by the website and a postal newsletter. As was already documented by Tauber (ibid. 1999: 65), financial sustenance was difficult as the sources of income were limited to membership fees, eventual entrance fees for events and the sale of beverages.

Almost ten years after Tauber's research the composition of the members of the Kulturverein had altered immensely. At the end of the 1990s about 40 or 50% of the members were Iranian Armenians, 20% from Lebanon or Syria, 20% from Turkey, while Armenians from the Republic were neither active nor present (Tauber 1999: 66). In contrast, the latter now were said to constitute probably half of the members, followed by the Iranian Armenians who made up about a third. Western Armenians from Turkey, Lebanon and Syria made up about 20%[9]. Still, the composition of present members was presumably not equivalent to those who paid membership fees. These were said to be mainly Diaspora Armenians. According to a long-term member of the Kulturverein, the increased participation of Republic Armenians in the community life of the Kulturverein had started about five years ago. Moreover, for two or three years now, about half of the members of the steering committee were said to be from the Republic of Armenia.

---

[9] Concerning the descendants of the first generation of Armenian immigrants who had come in the early 20th century and who are called "Deutsch-Armenier" (German Armenians) in the community, Tauber already asserts that these were not active community members in the end of the 1990s and were hardly known by the other community members (Tauber 1999: 72). During my research this group was not mentioned by any of my respondents.

In the history of the association, successive waves of migration with different causes and origins had repeatedly led to internal conflicts. Until the 1990s, the linguistic divide between the speakers of Eastern Armenian (Iran) and Western Armenian (Turkey, Lebanon, Syria) as well as the different prioritisation of identity markers with regard to the question of what it needs to be a "real" Armenian raised contention: Due to their living situation in Turkey, where the Armenian language was hardly sustainable and the church took the role of the saviour of Armenian identity, Turkish Armenians primarily identified themselves as Armenians through their adherence to the Apostolic Armenian Church. In contrast, Iranian Armenians perceived the command of the Armenian language as a primary marker of Armenian identity. In 1990/91, a certain degree of amalgamation of the groups was achieved, which became apparent in the mixed steering committee. With the onset of the migration wave from the Republic of Armenia at the beginning of the 1990s, these migrants were perceived as the new "Others" in the community by the resident Diaspora Armenians[10]. In the first years, Republic Armenians hardly visited the association, but they became more active as they had stayed in Hamburg for a longer time. Still, internal conflicts, now especially between Diaspora and Republic Armenians, remained an issue. Different habits and ways of conduct, which were ascribed to cultural differences, caused problems and, among others, resulted in the withdrawal of long-term members.

During her research Tauber observed that the organizational life of the community was characterised by a low level of activities and small amount of visitors. Her informants indicated pessimistic visions of the future of the community, its institution and the maintenance of Armenianness as "de facto" Armenian community life had come to a halt (Tauber 1999: 92). This was due to several problems the association then had to cope with: financial problems; steady flux of members due to re-migration; heterogeneity and internal cleavages; huge geographical dis-

[10] This strong internal differentiation is the reason why, in the following chapters, I will mainly differentiate my informants by these labels, i.e. "Republic Armenian" and "Diaspora Armenian". Thus, as will become clear, I do not intend to follow already present divides between these groups, but rather to show the similarities between them.

tance between member households and the association as well as the progression of assimilation (ibid. 1999: 65-66, 93). Although these problems had not been resolved according to a long-term member the situation had changed insofar as the level of activity by the Kulturverein had risen in the year of 2007. Regular activities offered comprised an Armenian language course, a choir group and a folk dance group for children and teens. Cultural events were organized – sometimes several times in a month – including performances of the dance group and the choir on different occasions as well as the invitation of the local Armenian boxing stars Susianna Kentikian and Artur Grigorian and classical and pop singers from Armenia. Due to the presence of Republic Armenians in the steering committee, cultural contacts with Armenia had increased and facilitated the arrangement of performances by artists from Armenia. These events were well attended and also drew Turkish and Iranian Armenians to the association. Another plan of the community concerned the organization of extra tuition by Armenian students for the Armenian youngsters, especially those who were deprived from planning their future and receiving proper education as they lived under the restricted circumstances of suspended deportation. The Kulturverein also organized events on the occasion of the 24th April, the official commemoration day of the genocide as well as the Independence Day of the Republic of Armenia (21st September) and the day of the death of Hrant Dink (19th January). Another aim was to build an Armenian church of one's own. In July 2007, the Kulturverein launched an appeal among the Armenians by spreading money transfer forms for donation via mail. On the 1st May 2008 donations had reached 5,729€[11].

Some of my respondents who originated from diaspora communities in the Middle East were critical about the development and the offerings of the Kulturverein. They were dissatisfied with the low level of cultural and social life, which did not meet their idea of an Armenian club life they had got used to in their respective countries of origin. Critique was also pointed to the fact that since the last wave of

---

[11]The amount and increase of donations was publicised on the website of the *Kulturverein*. Names of the donators were not given (Armenischer Kulturverein zu Hamburg e.V. n. y. b).

migration the association got more and more used by immigrants from Armenia who had problems with their precarious legal status. According to my observation, the accommodation was mainly appropriated by a group of women from the Republic and their kids. As Tauber also noticed, before the founding of Kilikia, the Kulturverein was hardly frequented by young people between 13 and 25 years old (ibid. 1999: 65). Also during my research especially the male youths were neither active nor present. A dozen of girls in their teens or early twenties who were active in the dance group and the choir usually performed at the cultural events offered by the Kulturverein. Older members ascribed the low participation of youth to a lack of interest in Armenian cultural life as well as to an advanced assimilation in the Christian German society.

The Kulturverein was linked to three further institutions: It was an official member of the Zentralrat der Armenier in Deutschland. It was also a member of the German association *Arbeitsgemeinschaft christlicher Kirchen in Hamburg* (Consortium of Christian Churches in Hamburg) used for ecumenical cooperation. Other constant relations existed with the Diocese of the Armenian Apostolic Church, which has its seat in Cologne. While the Kulturverein was a member of the former association for more than 15 years (see Grünberg et al. 1994: 54), it did not join the Diocese officially. However, a number of members of the Kulturverein were organized in the Diocese on a private level. The Kulturverein had the permission of the Diocese to organize church services in the Protestant church St. Gertrud in Uhlenhorst. According to statements, stable relations to other Armenian communities in Germany were almost non-existent. Regarding the position in the organizational landscape in Germany the association perceived itself as rather insignificant in general, though it was said to have lately gained a good reputation among the Armenian communities in Germany by its immediate organization of a demonstration after the murder of Hrant Dink in 2007. Contacts to other communities on the international level were said to be even less important. The contact to Armenia was limited to the invitation of artists for cultural events.

In August 2007, some youths who met in the Kulturverein founded their own youth organization named *Armenischer Jugendverband Kilikia e.V.* (Armenian youth association Kilikia), or abbreviated: Kilikia[12]. The members met monthly, every first Friday, in the centre of the Kulturverein. It was accessible on the internet by a website of its own where it also posted upcoming events (see Armenischer Jugendverband Kilikia e.V. n. y. a). The basic financial income of the organization was generated by membership fees.

Among others, the motivation to found Kilikia emanated from the dissatisfaction of the youth with the offers of the Kulturverein for youngsters. The number of members increased quickly within six months up to 40 (Armenischer Jugendverband Kilikia e.V. n. y. c). The members originated largely from the Republic of Armenia, while there were few Diaspora Armenians. In comparison to the Kulturverein, here the group of active teens and twens seemed to be more or less gender-balanced. The founding of Kilikia indicates that neither a general lack of interest in Armenian life nor advanced assimilation in the Christian German society were necessarily the reasons why the Armenian youths had not participated in the community life of the Kulturverein. The goals of the statutes of Kilikia resembled the goals of typical Armenian cultural organizations being concerned with the local sustenance and dissemination of Armenian culture and tradition among the youth. According to the statutes of Kilikia, further official goals were the promotion of youth activities in the area of culture, education and leisure time, the communication and cooperation with other youth organizations, especially those with similar missions as well as the integration of Armenian youth via participation in social and political life (Armenischer Jugendverband Kilikia e.V. n. y. b).

Kilikia offered regular activities (e.g. a drama group) as well as sporadic cultural and social events, mainly, but not only for its own peer group. Although it was independent from the Kulturverein, they shared the same accommodation, which

[12] The name "Kilikia" obviously refers to the last Armenian kingdom, which was constituted by Armenian migrants on the southern coast of present-day Turkey from 1080 to 1375 AD.

they began to renovate. Kilikia supported the Kulturverein by creating and maintaining a web site for their representation and also cooperated with it for the organization of social events like the commemoration of the day of death of Hrant Dink. In April 2008, they used their performance of a theatre play to raise donations for the support of an orphanage in Armenia. Also, Kilikia planned to organize translocal events similar to the nation-wide youth gathering "Jugendtreff" of the youth section *Junge Armenier* (Young Armenians) of the ZAD and to connect to Armenian youth in other communities in Northern Germany, particularly, the Armenian youth in Berlin.

Diaspora elites

Tölölyan defines diaspora elites or diasporists as individuals who belong to the "diasporic faction of the economic, political and cultural elites" and are involved in the discursive and non-discursive (re-)production of the diasporic culture and collective identity. Thus, on the one side they contain and guard the imagined boundaries of the community in the face of the host society, but also act as vanguards of change in the diasporic discourse (Tölölyan 2000: 109-110). According to Tölölyan, these diasporic forces are not concerted, but rather compete on what is the valid image of the diaspora to be disseminated, its true aims etc. Diasporists can be found among "journalists, intellectuals, teachers, scholars, activists, artists, performers, and entertainers", who may rely on organizations and institutions of the diaspora, which back them by support (ibid. 2000: 109).

When asking about outstanding individuals who were considered proactive forces in the development and sustenance of diasporic life and discourse in Germany or Hamburg, knowledge correlated with diasporic activity of the respective informant. Informants who were not involved in diasporic work were ignorant of any outstanding diasporic actor. Informants who were involved in organizational work and networking named in total nine "diasporists". Two names were mentioned by all respondents: the Armenian archbishop of Cologne and the founder of a research institute on genocide and diaspora. Further individuals named were an Armenian priest; an Armenian editor of a quarterly German-Armenian publication; an Armenian member of the ZAD who had been the main organizer of youth activities; a female member of the ZAD who had organized Armenian youth camps in Germany and Armenian language lessons for children for many years; a young Armenian scholar who was dedicated to academic research on the history of Armenians in Germany; a German-Armenian who had founded the German section of a charitable fund which supported Armenia and Arzach. With regard to the community in Hamburg, only one individual was mentioned, who was organized in the Kulturverein and was busy in organizing political events and lobbying.

According to one respondent none of these persons was extraordinarily wealthy. Rather they belonged to the cultural, religious and political elite, which had added to cultural sustenance and infrastructure of the Armenian diaspora in Germany. As the interviewee suggested the Armenian diaspora elite in Germany did not go hand in hand with the Armenian economic elite in Germany:

> "Well, there are some rich Armenians who are not included in my list [of diasporists] […] because they are not active in terms of being Armenian."

According to my information there were several economically powerful families who were said to be involved in financial support of diasporic matters, which aimed especially at the recognition of and public information on the genocide: The stone cross monument in Bremen (see also 5.3), the Dashnak party and the publication of a book on the genocide. One of them planned to establish a philanthropic foundation to support the development of Armenia. However, although my informant acknowledged that some individuals of the economic elite were willing to contribute sporadically by financing Armenian projects, they did not fulfill his notion of a proactive Armenian in terms of a diasporic.

The denial of the status "diasporist" to these individuals by my informant does not necessarily mean that they were not acting as diasporists. The exclusion, which my informant made, may rather be interpreted as a critique and hints at potential fractures within the milieu of diasporists: Although monetary potency existed in the diaspora, it apparently did not reach the local community structures, which my informant assumed as eminent for the sustenance of the Armenian diaspora and which were chronically under-financed. My hypothesis is that, among other reasons, the economic elite considered those local projects not profitable enough in the sense of a status gain, as their character would have been less visible to a greater public audience as, for example, a stone cross monument or the founding of a charitable fund.

Furthermore, it remains to be examined to what extent the role of diasporists was partly "outsourced" to German actors. Apart from the Deutsch-Armenische Gesellschaft, which I already introduced, there are historical examples of fervent German advocates of Armenian interests: For example, Armin T. Wegner who was mentioned by one of my informants in this context. Armin T. Wegner was an author and journalist who had witnessed the genocide in 1915 and 1916 and, back in Germany, publicized the atrocities against the Armenians and acted as their advocate. Together with other prominent non-Armenian supporters of the Armenians like Henry Morgenthau, Franz Werfel and Johannes Lepsius he received a symbolic grave on the plot of the memorial of the genocide in Yerevan (Hofmann 2005: 52). Also in recent times Armenian relations to German producers of scientific or public discourse (e.g. journalists, university professors) seem to have gained a high value: Recent commemorations of the 24th April of the ZAD and the Diocese in Frankfurt included the invitation of several German intellectuals, journalists and politicians as orators. In 2008, also the Kulturverein announced to invite several Germans intellectuals to speak at the annual commemoration. With regard to this phenomenon of German-Armenian cooperation, similar observations were made by Schwalgin during the official commemorations in Thessalonica and Athens: Publicly well-known and influential Greek individuals (academics and politicians) were invited to act as main orators. Based on the perception of a common experience as victims of the Turkish deportations and massacres at the beginning of the 20th century, those speeches demonstrated solidarity and support between the Greek and the Armenians (Schwalgin 2004: 135-136). The German speeches also construed a historical common ground, although in this case it was of a more asymmetrical character: The genuine responsibility towards the Armenian cause was usually deduced from Germany's role as a perpetrator of the Jewish Holocaust.[13]

5.2 Economic strategies

In order to detect the role of the diaspora in economic strategies I examined whether economic strategies relied on ethnicity, specific "ethnic" assets, or could be assumed to be specific middleman practices: Ethnic consumerism, intra-ethnic and inter-ethnic cooperation, self-employment, and the identification and exploitation of ethnic niches (see Basu 2006).

Ethnic entrepreneurship and economic niches

Data on the economic structure of the diaspora was hard to get. At the time of my research, Armenian economic life was almost invisible in the public sphere as well as, for example, in the Yellow Pages. Indicators for Armenian origin like the suffix "-ian" in the last name were not a common appearance in the names of businesses or shops. In this respect, the Armenian community differs for example from other resident migrant communities like the Turkish or Ghanaian, whose businesses and shops are easily identifiable in the public. Two shops, one second-hand shop and one shop dealing with Armenian souvenirs, were known by my informants. These were named after geographical Armenian regions or sites in the historical area of Armenian settlement, thus revealing their ethnic origin only to Armenians or connoisseurs of Armenian culture.

[13] For orators and speeches from 2004, 2005, 2007 and 2008 see the online archive of the ZAD (Zentralrat der Armenier n. y. a).

While, for example, the Turkish community's resident and economic pattern may arguably be perceived to form an "ethnic enclave"[14] in several quarters of German cities, this cannot be said for the Armenians in Hamburg. Apart from one shop which dealt with Armenian souvenirs there was no hint on small businesses which relied on ethnic goods and ethnic consumerism. One respondent explained to me that there had been Armenians in Hamburg who had tried their hands on selling ethnic goods, but that it failed as an economic strategy. One reason was the lack of clients and as my interviewee suggests the quick adaption to the new environment:

> "In the beginning when this was tried out there weren't many Armenians here and so it was left for the time being and later - when there were many Armenians here - they integrated well. Well, I also observe that in the courts, even when they come from other countries, they are well integrated in the European way. And they get their goods from somewhere else, for example, when they travel [...]."

The lack of spatial concentration of Armenians in Hamburg may also have added to the difficulties of sustaining small businesses for ethnic goods. Informants told me that alternative ways to obtain Armenian goods were, firstly, Turkish shops, where groceries were similar, or, as a second option, an import-export firm in Hamburg, which also traded products from Armenia. Furthermore, the opening of a small ethnic businesses itself was not perceived as a worthwhile goal, for it was seen as petty and unprofitable. When I asked an informant why there were not

[14] An ethnic enclave is marked by a residential clustering of an ethnic group in a neighbourhood and an economic orientation on ethnic goods and services of the given group. Thus ethnic enclavement can be seen as one possibility for ethnic entrepreneurship, which draws on co-ethnics as market, i.e. economic resource (Basu 2006: 586). Still, the critical population threshold regarding the absolute size and spatial concentration of a given ethnic group, which will result in the building of ethnic facilities is not clarified yet (see Schönwälder&Söhn 2007: 14). With regard to mono-ethnic concentration in German urban cities and quarters Schönwälder and Söhn ascertain that, generally, urban quarters with a high concentration of migrants (above 30%) tend to be multi-ethnic and that mono-ethnic concentrations above 10% are rare (ibid. 2007: 17, 20).

any Armenian restaurants or shops that offered specific Armenian goods, he responded:

> "I think it fails due to several reasons. Firstly, there are the costs, which are connected to the purchase of the goods, secondly, there are the legal requirements, which have to be met, that means, the tax office and all these authorities. Furthermore, the people who have the financial capital don't want to do this arduous work and the people who want to do this arduous work don't have the capital. I wouldn't do it, it's too laborious. The profit margin is so meagre that you - well, instead of this work you could do something else."

Another interviewee's comment suggests that the avoidance of small businesses was also a question of attitude:

> "Only education will push you forward - you can forget about everything else! No Döner[15] shop, no snack shop, none! These are all things for today and tomorrow."

Thus small ethnic businesses stood in opposite view to the rather high educational level of the Armenians, which was asserted by my informants (see 6.1). In sum, my observations were similar to those of Talai on the economic structure of the Armenian community in London, which - being a rather recent, decentralized, but institutionalized community of heterogeneous origin in a Christian country – resembles the community in Hamburg: According to her, Armenians "muted" their ethnic origin in business, tended to opt for self-employment and did not cater the needs of their co-ethnics by offering certain goods (Talai 1986: 254-255).

Although the first respondent claimed that initial ignorance of and difficulties with strict bureaucratic and judicial provisions in Germany impeded entrepreneurship,

---

[15] Popular Turkish snack in Germany and widespread ethnic business niche of the Turkish community.

it was still pursued by many Armenians. One of my respondents from the Republic of Armenia, an entrepreneur himself, maintained that the striving for self-employment was characteristic of the diaspora and not of Armenians in general. The tendency towards entrepreneurship and the idea of entrepreneurship as a feature of the diaspora was also supported by Tauber. According to her research about 20% of the Armenians were self-employed. Still, the majority was employed as workers, while others were working as artisans/craftsmen, retail dealers, merchants, employees and academics (Tauber 1999: 52).

To what extent Armenians occupied specific ethnic economic niches cannot be clarified here. Nevertheless, certain occupations seemed to be significant and to be connected to the diasporic living situation. Armenians were usually raised in a multi-lingual environment. This was not only true for the Diaspora Armenians, but also for the Armenians from the Republic or other ex-Soviet states who had been raised bilingually, with Russian as a second language. At the same time, learning languages was held in high esteem. Thus, most Armenians were in command of several languages, in some cases up to six or seven. Some had discovered their polyglot upbringing as a profitable asset, when huge migration flows from the former USSR started in the 1990s. German authorities such as the courts, the aliens department and the police urgently needed translators and interpreters to handle the mass of cases of immigrants and asylum seekers with, for example, Russian and Armenian background. Armenians were then approached for their linguistic competence and some of them seized the chance to become certified interpreters (Ger.: *Vereidigter Dolmetscher*). For some this had built the basis for self-employment.

As Tauber reports, several Armenians were able to make use of their contacts to their home country as well as of their language competence in the import-export business (ibid. 1999: 52). Nevertheless, one of my informants stated that only a small percentage of Armenians in Hamburg (2 to 5%) was engaged in the import-export business. According to him this low percentage was also due to the relatively high number of Republic Armenians in Hamburg who mostly had come as refugees and neither had experience in trade nor starting capital.

A further prominent employment option in Hamburg but also in general was said to be the trade of goldsmithing – a trade claimed to be a traditional Armenian one. Though I was told that there were a lot of Armenian goldsmiths in Hamburg and other cities of Germany I did not meet any. Their visibility in public was also said to be very low as many of them were from Turkey and did not display their Armenian last name or they had to have it changed into a Turkish one in Turkey. In this context it has to be mentioned that trades and crafts such as goldsmith, shoemaker or tailor etc. are collaterally documented as salient as Armenian economic niches in several accounts and seem to play an important role during the settlement of first generations of Armenians in the diaspora (Ter-Minassian 1988: 206; Brednikova et al. 1997: 57; Ordukhanyan 2005: 229; Mirak 1997: 395). An according economic strategy, which seemed to be implemented by several Armenians, was based on the combination of training and academic education: Some of my informants had learned a trade or craft in their youth – for example, by working in their father's business – and later went for academic education. As I was told by a Republic Armenian, this strategy was also followed by Armenians in Armenia to cushion unfavourable economic trends: Many Armenians who could not succeed with their academic title on the market switched to crafts. To what extent this strategy was implemented in Germany and Hamburg cannot be ascertained here.

Social networks in the economic sphere

Most of my informants were working in a mainly non-Armenian environment. This observation was also made by Tauber (ibid. 1999: 52). In general, sociability and social networks were perceived as important assets in a working life. Nevertheless, a relevance of social contacts to other Armenians in working life was usually negated. According to my informants, intra-Armenian contacts mainly existed in their private life. Pre-migration contacts to Armenians in Hamburg were almost non-existent. One informant explained that intra-Armenian contacts in the community in general were mostly relevant in the phase of settling down and primarily soothed the feeling of cultural alienation and did not serve as an economic resource:

> "Well, in the beginning diaspora certainly plays an important role, in the sense that it gives you the feeling of being at home, the feeling of having your own culture and not being foreign, to be understood, that certainly helps a lot in the initial stage. During the stage of integration you certainly look for the best qualities of the other culture and try to assess them – whether they are positive or negative. And in the last possible stage, integration has taken place or is completed. Then diaspora certainly is only of importance in certain contexts, that means: with regard to certain projects, events, [...] issues"

Institutions for the gathering of Armenian professionals like business clubs were said to be non-existent in Hamburg. Nonetheless, intra-Armenian cooperation in the economic sphere existed. According to the information I got, cooperation was more likely to exist in vertical employment relationships (employer and employee) or asymmetrical relationships (e.g. business and client) than in horizontal partner relationships (business partners). I heard of two enterprises, where co-ethnics were employed, in one case it was said that Armenians constituted a significant part of the work force. In another case the employment of Armenians was reasoned as a starting support for immigrated Armenians who still had to establish themselves economically:

> "Due to our profession we are very international, but we also have a lot of Armenians and we have supported a lot of Armenians in the beginning, that means when they were new here and didn't know how they could make a living here. Then we supported them, we trained them and also introduced them to [our profession] and thereby we also gave financial support."

One respondent had also been employed by an Armenian-led enterprise when he was rather new in Hamburg and in need of employment. An Armenian friend of his who already worked there had acted as the broker. To what extent the decision to employ co-ethnics was due to the idea of co-ethnical support or business-led rationale cannot be concluded here. In contrast to that, the cooperation as business partners was said to be difficult in general. One respondent stated:

> "This is paradox to me. On the one side the Armenians always try to stick together, but when you do some business for example: Armenians have much more hassle with each other than Armenians with other peoples. For example, Armenians and Russians, Armenians with someone else: There is much more subordination, I don't know whether the Armenian is then superior or the other way round, I don't know, but it works better."

The lack of cooperative behaviour among Armenians was uttered by several, but not all informants explicitly. Especially Armenians from the Republic complained about this behaviour and ascribed it to the distinct individualism among Armenians, which was as one informant put it "pulled through with elbows". A concrete example was reported by a respondent when he once attempted to recruit partners for his business idea:

> "[...] especially the Armenians from Armenia are not prepared to cooperate with each other in business. I have also suggested an acquaintance of mine to build up a business together and, because I had been busy in a different trade before, of course, I didn't have such a large clientele at this time. He said: 'No, you are weak now and we have plenty of orders, what is the incentive for me?' He wanted – not today anymore, but in the first years – to present himself as a big rival. Well, today it is a relation like an elephant to an ant concerning the size of turnover and the position on the market. But back then I had suggested it to him and he didn't want to, because - according to him - my order situation was weaker than his."

Though Armenians were said not to team up as partners to found businesses, co-operation on common projects between co-ethnics coming from different branches obviously existed in other spheres.

Concerning business fruitful relations to Germans also existed. Support of Germans appeared in different shapes during my research, such as mental support and adviser in decision making and bureaucratic matters during the start-up phase of a business or as concrete partnering. The latter was the case when a German business man acted as a partner of an Armenian immigrant who could not start a business himself due to the restrictions which came with his residence status. Thus, decisions in entrepreneurial relations seemed to be made on the ground of pragmatic considerations – especially with regard to impeding context factors. One interviewee, for example, declared it one of his entrepreneurial principles to entrust "ethnic" experts with specific tasks or fields so that, for example, German issues would be left to German employees.

5.3 The urban environment

I further wanted to find out whether Hamburg as an urban space had had a special meaning for my interviewees' decision to migrate. Did Hamburg – as a port city - offer certain conditions which were favourable, for example, with regard to economic establishment, aspects of Armenian community life etc.? Most of my informants did not perceive the choice of Hamburg as a place of settlement as a conscious decision. Most of them called their choice of Hamburg a mere coincidence. Only one of my informants chose Hamburg for its logistic advantage as a port city. One interviewee argued that Hamburg as a destination was not very attractive to many Armenians as it lacked a firm Armenian institutional infrastructure and cultural life. Therefore, they would tend to migrate further to more developed communities.

The reasons why my informants decided to migrate can often not be put into one word, as direct and indirect causes and triggers can be diverse and intermingled. In several cases, the motive for migration was the pushing of one's professional career, i.e. they came for a working contract or to pursue their studies. In some cases the insecure political conditions in the home country was mentioned as a reason for migration as well as the well-being of the family. (Familial) chain migration was non-existent among my interviewees.

Significant places – The stone cross in Bremen

Searching for meaningful institutions and places for the Armenian community in Hamburg it became clear that, apart from the accommodation of the Kulturverein, the only place of significance mentioned was the Protestant St. Gertrud's church in Uhlenhorst. In agreement with the German parish, the Armenians used it for the celebration of religious events. Interestingly, several Armenians in Hamburg referred also to the "Kreuzstein" (stone cross, Arm.: *khachkar*) in Bremen as a place of importance. The stone cross is a genuine Armenian artefact, which bears witness to the merging of Christian-Armenian cultures for over 1100 years. Stone crosses were erected "everywhere Armenians had lived" (Hofmann, 1997b: 206; translation by C.T.) and for multiple purposes: as part of religious edificial culture, as memorials for a person or a historical event.

photo 1 The stone cross in Bremen. Photo by Caroline Thon.

The stone cross had been erected on a green behind the Central Station of Bremen in 2005 (see photo 1). Officially, the *Stiftung Armenisches Kulturerbe* (Foundation for Armenian cultural heritage) in Luneburg had sponsored this project (Rosenfelder 28.07.2005: 13). A stone cube next to the monument bears the Armenian and German inscription: "On the occasion of the 90th anniversary of the genocide of the Armenians in the Ottoman Empire we commemorate 1,500,000 Armenians who were murdered" (see photo 2). The stone cross, one respondent stated, attracted many Armenians from outside of Bremen on the commemoration day of the genocide, i.e. on 24th April. All Armenians with whom I talked about the monument ascribed a symbolic value to its existence and the event of its erection. My research suggests that it was a symbolic marker of the establishment of Armenians in the public consciousness as a cultural group with a specific concern.

The stone cross in Bremen was the first one located in the German public space. As such, it was the task of the German municipality to take care of it and, for example, to remove Turkish graffiti - a fact, which one interviewee stressed as an important feature. Also, it was hoped that the monument would raise awareness of the genocide in the non-Armenian public. For that reason, the fact that the official erection had been mainly attended by Armenians and Turks who formed a counter-demonstration, was regretted by one Armenian:

"[...] there were almost only Armenians and this, this was the thing that bothered me a bit, because – ok, it is fantastic – but I mean on the occasion of the 24th April I can go somewhere to a commemoration. Thereby, I won't learn anything new, thereby, my attitude won't change, I know about that. The important thing is that the others learn more about it."

Another informant called it a symbol for a new German policy towards the Armenians and the Armenian-Turkish conflict over the recognition of the genocide. Apart from the meaning of the monument in the context of identity politics and public position of the Armenians in the majority society, one interviewee hoped that it also would set an example to the future generation of the diaspora and would foster their activity:

photo 2 Inscription next to the cross stone in Bremen (Photo by Caroline Thon).

"[...] the most important effect this [stone cross] had, or perhaps has or will have, is that in the community, [...] that the young people will pull themselves together and that they see: 'Aha! If you are active, such things are possible.' That it serves as a symbol – that is most important to me."

The erection of a stone cross monument as a truly Armenian artifact was perceived as a victory in identity politics in the public sphere.

6 The cultural concept of success

In this chapter I will discuss the existence of a concept of success among the Armenians in the diaspora. Such a concept can be understood in terms of "cultural knowledge", i.e. values, norms and convictions shared by a specific group (Kokot 1992: 368). Therefore, I will draw on perceptions about "how to become successful", "resources of success", "being successful" and the "characteristics of successful Armenians". I will introduce the most salient notions and will also show as far as possible inhowfar these values and norms were translated into action and practices.

It also must be mentioned that the success model, which I will depict here, cannot be considered static, monolithic or unambiguous, but part of a discourse. According to my observations, notions of what it takes to be considered a successful *Armenian* were partly, but not fundamentally, contested. Moreover, individual success had two dimensions of reference: The Armenian family and the Armenian nation. While the basis of individual success was laid in the realms of the family, success had to be legitimised by the Armenian collective. The dimension of the host society was also crucial as it set the context factors, which, for example, determined the possibility of agency and social mobility of the diasporic group.

The model emanated entirely from data of individuals who were at least partly able to gear their life towards this success model. My study does not cover Armenians who were living under precarious conditions due to their migration status as asylum seekers or undocumented migrants. According to my informants, these Armenians differed in their habitus and therefore also in their notions of success. This perceived divide is discussed in an excursus in chapter 6.2. Finally, I will illustrate to what extent the Armenian community in Hamburg was judged "successful" by its members and what was perceived as needed for a full communal establishment.

The diasporic narrative and cultural legacies

Before going into matters of notions of individual success and success as a community, I want to point to the presumable cognitive basis of notions of success. In order to deduce values and strategies, which were connected with success, my respondents drew on the topos of "a mobile people without a state" or, alternatively, a (persecuted) minority dependent on the good will of the alien majority society. According to some of my informants, the status as a mobile people and minority was associated with multiple insecurities. An often-used expression for this state of existence was "under pressure":

> "Of course it is always like that: When you belong to a small people there is always a bit of pressure. That is normal. You always want to show that you are competent, probably. You can explain it like this. And there is always this ambition, if you know from history, that the Armenians were persecuted first and then your parents, your grandparents - they have lost everything. [...] And then they emigrated. You also realise all that as a child. [...] my grandparents have told me how that they had to leave everything behind. Or my father had [been] almost [killed?] like many of the relatives who were dead or were killed. And at the age of six or seven he remained all on his own in East Turkey and had to emigrate all alone and then he came to Jerusalem. As a young child. And then he had to make his way in life. And when you hear about that, how it happened in the past and that your parents didn't have anything, but went on nevertheless, then you say: 'now I have to make proper use of what I got now' and then you have the opportunity to progress and then you try to do more than average [...]." (Diaspora Armenian)

> "Well, Armenians have a quality, which can be found all over the world in minorities like the Jews or others: That they have become very flexible due to the experience of expulsions and this has been passed on over the generations. So, flexibility also means the degree of adaptability in any society and also societal structure [...] it is inherent in the Armenians and the small

> peoples, which have often been expelled that they always have to adapt to the new conditions and that they have also learned, recognized and also, partly, applied the values. So, that is an important part of the success in every country where you dwell, especially in the diaspora." (Armenian from the Republic of Armenia)

Thus, this fundamental diasporic experience was supposed to be the root and motor for the development of certain values and strategies, which will be mentioned below.

The topos of the experience as a persecuted and mobile minority in a foreign society is, according to Hofmann, generally monopolized by the Diaspora Armenians and conceptualized as the basic experience of "Diaspora-Armenianness" (Arm: *spyurkahatyutyun*); as such it is bound to a specific mentality of balanced open-mindedness, adaptability and conservatism. In contrast, the recently emigrated Republic Armenians are seen as deprived from this experience and, thus, of a cosmopolite attitude and sensitivity towards the perils of assimilation (Hofmann 1997b: 165). According to my research this broadly agreed-upon cultural dichotomy of Diaspora Armenians and the "sedentary" Armenians from the Republic of Armenia was not valid. As can be seen in the second exemplary quotation above, the diasporic narrative was also claimed by Republic Armenians as a cultural basis of their success model, in spite of the rather short duration of their diasporic experience and, in some cases, the absence of any involvement in the institutionalized diasporic community. However, as I observed, this topos was embedded in slightly different narratives – e.g. depending on whether one descended from a family whose migration was triggered by the genocide or not. The former group usually told it with reference to the expulsion and the human calamity, which took place in their own family history. In contrast, the latter often referred to the general experience of repetitive expulsions in Armenian history. One of my informants, a descendant of refugees of the genocide, described this event as having imposed a historical imperative to survive as a continuous force in his life:

> "I have taken the Armenian way: 'I have to survive'. That means, everywhere we live we always have this problem: We have to survive, we have to exist somehow. Sometimes you are tired of that. You say: 'how much energy do I further have to waste on this?' A German doesn't need to waste this energy. He doesn't have this problem, right? Of course, if I want to be good at something then – in addition to this energy – I have to develop myself in a way that in comparison to the others I try to be a little bit better, so that I will be admitted into their society. And this requires a lot of discipline and energy. And this is the success of our diaspora and that some are successful in some countries to such an extent. [...] When I came here I had to learn everything anew. I calculated: I had lost ten years. Well, I cannot compensate these ten years, but I can try by my industriousness to achieve point X, which I would have achieved under normal circumstances, under these conditions, in my situation. That means I had to work ten years as if it were twenty. This I have done: in the time [span of ten years] I have succeeded in opening a firm alongside my studies."

"Survival" showed to be a repetitive term in many contexts of Armenian discourse. It penetrated different aspects of Armenian life and culture as an imperative, which stemmed from the diasporic experience. I suggest therefore that the leitmotif in the Armenian concept of success can be best understood as "survival". As different narratives suggest, the leitmotif of survival refers not only to the biological and physical survival with regard to the concrete experience of extinction by the genocide but it also can be understood in terms of cultural survival in a foreign society. This hypothesis corresponds with the widely known Armenian distinction between the biological "Red Genocide" and the cultural "White Genocide", which are central keywords in the active diasporic discourse – although I do not want to presume, that this discourse was shared by all of my informants. While the Red Genocide refers to the historical genocide committed by the Turks in 1915/16, the White Genocide denotes the threat of assimilation in the diasporic situation (especially in Christian countries and by means of exogamy) and, as its consequence, the disappearance of Armenian culture by assimilation (see Bakalian 1994: 2-3; Hofmann 1993: 109-112).

During my research, my interviewees characterized successful Armenians often as "natural fighters" who struggle themselves through any situation of hardship and who go for their aims. Concrete characteristics deduced from these perceptions, and which described the Armenian work ethic were mainly: Extraordinary industry, doggedness, flexibility and adaptability, imperturbable optimism, loyalty and honesty. In this context the character of the fighter as an individualist also appeared during my research as an apparently crucial criterion for the appreciation of achievement.

The quotation of my interviewee mentioned above also points out that the context of diasporic life was perceived to bear an immanent disadvantage when compared to life of the "sedentary" majority society. Beyond mere survival, this life demanded surpassing the average level in order to overcome the minority bias and to be able to progress. The idea of continuous progression will be tackled in the following chapters. In contrast to these assumed effects of living under diasporic conditions, values and norms linked with educational standards, appreciation of arts, music and languages, but also social competences, were rather associated with the general Armenian cultural heritage as such. Due to their early acquisition of an Armenian alphabet and script of their own, their autonomous national Christian Church, their cultural productiveness, their technical ingenuity and role as multi-lingual merchants of high esteem in history, they displayed a strong self-perception as a civilized people (see also Brednikova et al. 1997: 67).

6.1 The Armenian family - Generating success

My research supports the idea that the family is central in the Armenian concept of "success" and that individual success is intertwined with the Armenian notion of family in manifold ways. The forming of a family itself was identified as an essential aspect of "being successful". This is not to be understood in the pure terms of reproduction, which had, though, a very high value. Rather, my research supports Pattie's findings, who describes the Armenian family concept as promoting a balanced melange of reproduction, in terms of number of children, and the pursuit of values like "achievement (including education, business, or professional accomplishment), hospitality, acquisition, and display [...]" (Pattie 1997: 152). Furthermore, the family was perceived as an important basis for individual success, especially concerning the accumulation of cultural capital. It was striking that the usually discrete intra-familiar social "inheritance" of cultural capital, as it is termed by Bourdieu (ibid. 2005: 58), was a mechanism Armenians were very much aware of and which they cherished as an explicitly cultivated tradition.

The children - Education and achievement orientation

In her account on Armenian culture, Hofmann states that in the diaspora education has an outstanding value and is held in high esteem for its character as an ever-portable asset:

> "Diaspora Armenians are extraordinarily eager to gain education. They know that profound knowledge and a pronounced ability to learn is the most important mobile property, which can be taken everywhere in the case of flight from danger or persecution." (Hofmann 1993: 106; translation by C.T.).

This quote implies that the experience of mobility is deeply rooted in the awareness of the Armenian diaspora and that it serves as a foundation for the high regard of educational achievements[1]. The extraordinary valuation of education is supported by my research in general, but the statement has to be refined. Firstly, my findings show that norms and values fostering educational ambition were not necessarily bound to diasporic experience but could also be observed among the

[1] Although figures are never given, several accounts mention the above-average educational level of Armenians in the diaspora: e.g. Brednikova et al. 1997: 57; Aghanian 2007: 3.

shortly-before "sedentary" Armenians from the Republic of Armenia. By acknowledging the traditionally high level of education and the high quota of academic graduates in Armenia during the Soviet period, Diaspora Armenians also did not deny this asset to the Republic Armenians. Several informants maintained that the educational standard in the Republic of Armenia was superb.

Education, knowledge and striving for it as well as the dedication to language and multi-lingualism were identified as part of a general Armenian cultural heritage. One interviewee ascribed the high esteem for education to the scarcity of natural resources in Armenia and the concomitant need of specialization in human capital for survival:

> "[Armenia] has no natural resources you can sell, for example, and make a living from. You have to be clever, so to say, to survive. And this was always the reason why people always looked for education and perhaps always, also in the history of Armenia, went outside Armenia to learn something and then perhaps they came back, or they didn't."

Secondly, the transferability of education as capital – whether embodied or institutionalized – is threatened as soon as it is not recognized by the new "market". The recognition of academic titles, which were obtained in the country of origin, for example, could not be taken for granted and could, as I will show later on, result in a loss of status. Hence knowledge might be mobile, but its value or rather convertibility does not necessarily remain the same.

The importance of education and achievement in the realm of family (life) was strongly emphasized by my interview partners. Thereby the origin, i.e. the fact whether they belonged to the Diaspora Armenians or to the Armenians who recently immigrated from the Republic of Armenia or other former Soviet countries did not matter at all. Several fathers confirmed their high expectations towards the education of their children. It was not only excellence in school that was fostered, but parents also attached a lot of importance to the promotion of arts and music as well as languages as private hobbies. Several interview partners confirmed that families tended to promote their children's talents - or rather the talent of the most promising offspring - in school, arts and music or language skills eagerly. According to Bourdieu, this education in "legitimate", i.e. socially recognized arts in terms of learning to play a noble instrument or enjoying certain, e.g. classical, music or works of arts can be valued as a sublimation of an "educated middle-class" habitus and as the latter's most imposing distinction (Bourdieu 1982: 41). By competing with other families for such cultural assets, families raised their symbolic capital as one of my informants described:

> "Yes! Education! Education! Not only languages. Education and arts, education and arts! Armenian families show off: 'Look, how nicely my son plays the piano' and: 'Look, and my son can speak English perfectly, and French!' This is still being shown off with. Immensely!"

The display of children's talents was embedded in the concept of Armenian hospitality and took place in the guise of entertainment such as poetry recitation, musical performance etc. whenever guests entered the house. One interviewee evaluated this as a fundamental aspect of the Armenian way of education:

> "Well, as a child I had to play very often [...]: I and my sister, her playing the piano, me playing the flute and always the same programme for different audiences. But as you will certainly already have learned: Armenians say that Armenians are raised at a 'table of society', the children. Well, an enormous educational process takes place by the influence of society, by encounter, by demand."

Nonetheless, the acquisition of an academic degree, that means the institutionalization of the cultural capital, was of utmost importance. After graduation from school an academic degree was the primary and non-debatable goal. One student from the Republic of Armenia succinctly called it a "standard" among Armenians. As one Diaspora Armenian in his forties remembered:

> "My mother never demanded a birthday present from us, she never demanded a Christmas present. She told us kids then: 'When you bring me your certificate from university, then you have given me a present. And you may take the subject you want to. The academic education is for you, but the certificate is mine.' From my childhood on I knew I had to study."

Similar experiences were shared broadly among my other respondents. Also for Armenians who emigrated recently from the Republic the pursuit of academic studies was a must. Thus, the meaning of an academic degree or education in general is not only to be seen in economic terms, as Hofmann's quotation suggests. Besides its potential as economic capital, educational achievement was acknowledged as symbolic capital:

> "[...] yes, [the family] is rather like a clan [...] - the family wants to show how successful it is and then there are these kids being the show-pieces or something like that. So, that counts in some way if you tell someone: 'Oh look, my son, he has a fantastic job now' and things like that. And I think this is a kind of status symbol."

As my respondent suggested here, symbolic capital, which was gained in these social "competitions", was not individualized, but it radiated on the whole (extended) family. This phenomenon was also mentioned by Pattie, who did research among the Armenians on Cyprus: "Accomplishment in the educational sphere is usually individual, but this then reflects on or includes the larger family" (ibid. 1997: 179). My interviewee further added that family efforts were strategically accumulated on the most promising offspring(s). She also referred to the family as a "clan", which, in the context of the interview, implied the high importance of intra-familial bonds and the family network in the individual's life as such.

Lonely fighters and big spenders - Successful Armenians

The salient importance of altruistic contribution was also backed up by the results gained by free listing of Armenians considered successful. As free listing revealed a rather long column of particularistic statements, the more it was striking that one individual gained vote from all: Charles Aznavour. The French Armenian chansonnier was appreciated unanimously by Armenians of all origins and mentioned first in most of the lists, often with a touch of enthusiasm and pride. As two of my respondents said:

> I1: "Well, for me personally, frankly, Charles Aznavour was always the leader of the people." [...]
> I2: "He was the representation"
> I1: "Yes, for me he was the representation of the diaspora. In my eyes he has created perfection that means perfection concerning his success and the sharing of his success with his people, fighting for his people and therefore I deem him a 'perfect communication'."

It seems that Charles Aznavour not only provided "the perfect communication" between individual success and the well-being of the collective as one of the interviewees suggests. Moreover, Aznavour unified the Diaspora and Armenia by his biography and his effort in Armenian matters. Thus, he was perceived as *the* universal institution of identification for Armenians. This view was also stressed from the side of the Diaspora Armenians. Moreover, Aznavour established the *Aznavour for Armenia-Fund*. With his fund, Aznavour set the prime example in the humanitarian assistance of Armenia after the earthquake. His charitable organization had raised millions of dollars (Panossian 1998: 176). In addition to this role as an Armenian philanthropist and outstanding artist, Aznavour and his family typified the post-genocide "success story" or rather "survival story". His father, a pianist, was saved by the French fleet, which took 4,000 refugees from Musa Dagh[2] on board.

> "The father of Charles Aznavour was a piano teacher. As a young man he practically [...] fled with his family, he managed to survive, to get to Paris. Charles Aznavour was born in Paris and he really grew up with music, his mother being a singer, his father a piano teacher. And well, he became that Charles Aznavour. Or Sylvie Vartan, she was also Armenian. Her parents also managed to flee from Turkey. Many Armenians have done this, 180,000 have managed to escape, to go to Paris, with the help of the French and ships. Well, and they became such great artists!"

Thus, for this informant from the Middle East Charles Aznavour and his family signified not only the survival of the genocide by the people as such, but apparently also the resurrection of Armenian culture and excellence out of ruins. Moreover, he embodied the characteristics of a "fighter" – a picture that was here also tied to the survival of the genocide. Apart from this historical reference, the overcoming of apparently insurmountable obstacles, the managing of an extraordinary ascent by oneself, seemingly without external support, was held in high esteem. This characteristic of "pushing oneself through" which some identified as part of "individualism", was furthermore understood as an important and typical Armenian trait by several of my informants. Several economically successful interviewees also referred to this characteristic as they denied the existence of any help or influence - apart from their family - during their socio-economic ascent. Rather, their biographies were narrations of "self-made men", sometimes even "from rags to riches"-life stories - this did not exclude the fact that in some cases external support was mentioned at other points of the interview.

---

[2] The historical rescue of Armenian refugees from Musa Dagh at the seaside of Southern Turkey during the genocide also gained prominence and symbolic value by the novel of the Jewish author Franz Werfel "The forty days of Musa Dagh", first published in 1933 (Werfel [1933] 1978).

Aznavour was followed in recognition by Cherilyn Sarkissian (Cher), the US-pop singer, Kirk Kerkurian, owner of a business empire and major shareholder of Daimler Chrysler in the US and Andre Agassi, the international tennis champion from the US. While the appraisal of Aznavour was, among others, based on his self-identification as Armenian, Agassi's inclusion in the list was controversial for the opposite reason. He was accused by some of never having displayed his Armenian origin in public. For them the open and public reference and loyalty towards one's Armenian origin constituted an important criterion of being acknowledged as successful. With the exception of André Agassi, Charles Aznavour, Cher, and Kirk Kerkurian were again unified by and praised for their benevolent action. Besides his fund, Aznavour was said to have produced a film on the genocide massacres; Cher had financially supported the poor in Armenia; Kirk Kerkurian was the founder of the *Lincy Fund*, which is the main contributor of the *United Armenian Fund* (UAF). He was said to have taken an immense role in the development of Armenia by financing its reconstruction. These personalities were therefore seen as exemplary success stories and were idols for many of my interviewees.

Excursus: Aspects of gender

Although the general expectation towards achievement and education seemed to be independent from gender at the first glance, my research suggests that there was a qualitative difference in the fostering of daughters and sons. I formulate the hypothesis that girls' achievement served rather as symbolic capital in the cultural sphere, while the sons' achievement also had to pay off economically. Several interviews with female and male informants suggested that there was a traditional gender bias. As a female student originating from Yerevan stated, reproduction persisted to be the primary expectation towards girls in Armenia (see also Ishkanian 2002: 384) and that they were in general not supposed to enter the job market and transform this capital into economic gain. Thus, the education of girls remained first and foremost symbolic capital, though, in times of economic hardship, women also looked for work to contribute to the family's income.

Although I cannot say to what extent this also applied to Diaspora Armenian girls, the high expectations towards the economic achievement of the male children prevailed both among Republic and Diaspora Armenians. This was said to be due to aspects of traditional Armenian social organization where the youngest son was supposed to take care of the elderly parents. Traditionally, he stayed with his parents after his marriage. It was argued that this model was nowadays almost non-existent in urban, especially non-Armenian, environments. Also, one can easily imagine that migration was an obstacle to it. Nonetheless, the idea of the son as a caretaker of the parents persisted.

Male offspring were thus the main focus of parental ambitions. As a future head of the family they were taken special care of: On the one hand they were the focus of attention, on the other, their role was burdened with high expectations. This was particularly true for the father-son-relationship as one of my informants mentioned. One informant implied that the educational opportunities, which were offered to the sons by their parents, had to be paid back in such way that the family standard could be to sustained or – better - improved. As another respondent told me, the failure of the son to return the harvest of this seed to his parents meant a disaster for an Armenian father.

The lack of a male offspring though may result in the transfer of the son's role onto the daughter, as the example of one of my female respondents - an only child - indicated. Her father, who first preferred a male descendant, came to terms with the situation by pushing his daughter into the role of the missing son – nonetheless expecting from her the usual behavioural and reproductive role as a daughter. She expected these two roles to collide in the future:

> "[My father] always demands: 'Yes, you have to get a good job', but this somehow contradicts with his opinion; 'You should also have a good marriage'"

According to my informant, her status among the members of her extended family was also influenced by this shift in roles:

> "[... thereby] one's role changes in a way. Suddenly you are a kind of representative and you get a lot of admiration from your male cousins and so on [...] well, even if you are female and, thus, normally the one to be protected, you are then the one who is pushing forward."

This example indicates that traditional gender expectations and roles were handled with pragmatism and were adapted to the condition when it served the interest and the success of the family.

The generation contract - Reciprocity and progression

Two male informants explained educational ambition as what I will call a "silent intergenerational reciprocal contract". According to them, Armenian children were raised with the awareness of the toils and sacrifices their parents had made and with the sense of being an inseparable and responsible part of the family's fate. This put huge pressure on the child:

> "And therefore it was always clear to me that I am responsible for the whole and that I have my share. That means: My success is their success. This means a lot of pressure. As a child – if you are not only producing the pressure yourself, but your parents also put pressure on you – you know by then: If you fail somewhere than this failure will hurt your parents very much. That is a lot - that is a great burden [...]."

Nevertheless this aspect of the parent-child relationship was appreciated – both by younger and older respondents. It was acknowledged to be part of Armenian tradition where the awareness and striving for incorporated and institutionalized cultural capital would be passed on to future generations. It was perceived as an Armenian duty. The conviction that "the child will do likewise with his or her future children" was mentioned both by parents as well as young adults. One respondent who came from the so called Inner Diaspora called this the "chain":

> "[...] we don't turn around and thank our parents in terms that we say: 'Well, super, here you got your economic profit for what you have invested into us' – no. We say: 'Ok, we'll give the same love, the same affection to our kids. This is our duty and this is the chain, the cohesion."

As I will show in chapter 6.2, the meaning of the chain transcended the mere circle of the family. Rather, the notion of an intergenerational contract for future progression can be seen as part of a wider idea, namely, the creation of national elite.

The parents - Readiness to make sacrifices

The upbringing of the children was, as I already delineated above, a central topic of Armenian family life. The virtual future opportunities of the offspring built the core of family decision-making. As one respondent from the Caucasus put it:

> "[...] because all questions in the later life of an Armenian are grounded in, cumulate in this point: questions of relationships, marital problems, questions of career – all these issues are to be measured according to this point, that is: 'What – the priority being the family and the family being defined as the children – what is important for my children'?"

The children were not just seen as the future "capital" of the family, but they *were* the family. This was not just true in pragmatic decisions, but also in social relations, where they were deemed as the surface on which the capabilities and the assets of the family are visible to the public. Children were seen as a mirror of their parents. Therefore, high importance was attached to the commitment to and support of the children and supervision of their development. Two Armenian fathers I spoke to - one from the Republic of Armenia, one from the Middle East - invested their little free time or coffee breaks at work to support and also to control their children's achievement in school. One of these informants described the relation to his only son and his principles of education as follows:

> "When he brings home an 'E' I don't say it is always worse or if gets an 'A' I say that it is better. No! What do I offer, what do I demand? It is only about that. If I spend a lot of time with my child and he speaks three, four languages, the other fathers all go playing golf or tennis and I sit at home and teach my kid then I demand results for that. That is the difference. And in Armenia this is extreme! [...] But I have said at our home [...] the main thing is that you raise your child in the right way and therefore you have to have time for your child. You cannot raise a kid *en passant*: 'I go to drink a beer tonight, I have got my group of regulars and I've got no time for your school stuff'. This is not ok. If my son says: 'Dad, I need your help' then I have to be there, I have to put my work aside. The kid needs help? He will be helped. So. And when I see that I have helped him, I give him time: 'You have to learn'. I demand an answer, what he has gained from learning. And when I see that he can't concentrate then I have to find the reason: is it the notebook or the game computer? Then it will be taken away. I will call home five times a day: 'Is he playing or is he learning?' – I follow that. I leave my meeting for five minutes, I don't smoke, I call home: 'What is [my son] doing?' Like this. Perhaps [my son] will do the same with his kid."

This statement was echoed in similar ways explicitly and implicitly in several biographies of my informants. In some cases, parents or older siblings even assumed the role of the teacher, teaching their children or brothers and sisters for example English instead of, as one of my respondents put his experience, "teaching me to ride a bike".

The spectrum of sacrifices not only comprised spending time on extra-education or control. The proverb "The Armenians live for themselves until the birth of the first child; thereafter, they live for their children" implicated that starting a family was connected with a high degree of commitment. Having a child thus also meant taking decisions with a high impact on family life, for example, migration and/or loss of status for the parents. In at least two cases it was reported that the migration decision of the family was directly connected to considerations of the future prospects of the children: One family sought a safer political environment for their children, another had migrated in search of better educational opportunities for the offspring. In the latter case the father was an academic with three diplomas, when he decided to leave his home country with his family to enhance the chances of his only son. In exchange, he had to give up his own professional career, as his diplomas were not acknowledged in Germany. He entered a blue-collar job as a worker on construction sites and later opened his own small enterprise in this sector. According to his son, the status gap his father experienced was compensated by the potential gain for his son:

> "He was content with the opportunities his son had, regarding the learning of languages, perspectives and so on. That made him happy."

Others who, or whose families, migrated for reasons not obviously or explicitly connected with their children's future, confirmed that they (or their parents who had taken the decision to migrate) embraced the chance that their children would be raised in a foreign-language environment, which would naturally increase their (language) competences and, thus, their future perspectives.

The orientation and the purpose of this family practice were summed up by one young parent as follows:

> "[...] the main direction of success [is] that the children become more successful or may be wealthier – I don't know – or may be more famous than their parents. This is their recipe somehow."

Taking this higher aim into account the temporary or irreversible loss of status risked by some of my informants or their parents was exchanged for a delayed gratification.

6.2 The Armenian nation – Legitimizing success

As was already mentioned the accumulation of capital as such is not equivalent to success. Individual success is a product of the act of social recognition by the social environment. In the following chapter, I will illustrate that in this respect the Armenian nation played a crucial role as a further frame of reference. The success of the individual had to trickle down on the Armenian nation, it had to nourish the success of the collective. In the following it will be explained how this rather abstract notion was put into practice.

Reinvestment into the nation - Philanthropy and contribution

The readiness to make sacrifices was not restricted to the relationship between and parents and children; rather it was an important principle which encompassed the whole Armenian nation. In practice, making sacrifices meant acting philanthropic and making a contribution to the continuance of the Armenian people by donating either money or talent to it. Thus, the readiness to make sacrifices to the Armenian nation can be seen as one pillar of its survival[3]. Again it was striking that Diaspora Armenians and Armenians of the so called New Diaspora, i.e. from Armenia and the former Soviet countries, agreed over this principle.

"It is a shame when you have reached the heights and no one will be able to follow you". This saying was mentioned once, when I asked about Armenian philanthropy and its principles. My informant from the Caucasus further clarified:

> "That means that you have been selfish, that you have not drawn anybody with you and you didn't pass on your knowledge that you have gained [...] Among the Armenians it's like that: If you have achieved something then you look back and think: 'Who else could go with me? Who else could go this same way with me, at least as far as me?' And then there are Armenians who have exceeded their abilities and say: 'I have come this far, I cannot go any further, I will push the others further, because they have a lot more potential than me.'"

The idea to push the future generation, to nurture the chain of development, to transfer cultural capital, thus could also be identified in non-family contexts. On the one side this idea of elite sponsorship was realized by institutionalized support in the form of several Armenian foundations – among them, especially the Gulbenkian Foundation[4] in Portugal was often mentioned and praised. On the other side, sponsorship was arranged at the level of private patronage. Three of my respondents from Armenia and the Middle East had enjoyed the benefits of

---

[3] For the central meaning of sacrifice in Armenian community life see also Schwalgin&Sökefeld 2000: 4-5.

[4] Calouste Gulbenkian (1869-1955) is known as an Armenian oil tycoon, who was born in Istanbul, but later dwelled in Paris, London and – finally – Portugal. Posthumously, his fortune was invested in large part in the founding of the Gulbenkian Foundation, which is devoted to the promotion of arts, science, education and benevolence. Among its manifold activities and projects, which are not only directed toward Armenian needs, it grants scholarships and supports Armenian communities in its statutory fields with an annual budget of US $ 3.5 million (see Fundação Calouste Gulbenkian 2008).

sponsorship during their academic education in form of financial support – either by one of the Armenian philanthropic funds or by private persons. One of those who had been supported by the latter stated:

> "Sometimes [my situation] was so bad that I went to an Armenian in my home country who was the boss of the electric power company. Well, someone had told him [about me] and he was not married [...]. Then he supported me for one or two years. Well, sometimes you find people like that."

Another respondent experienced private sponsorship in his home country in the shape of an institutionalized support system called *san*, which refers to the relation between the godfather and the child to be baptized (Arm.: *sanik*). It had been initiated by the Gulbenkian Foundation, but afterwards it was organized locally by the church. His family received financial support for the children's school fees. My respondent's sponsor remained anonymous so that the family could not feel in debt towards anyone. This way of assistance still existed: The respective informant supported school children in Armenia via the Armenian Church.

The altruistic investment into the future elite was just one aspect of philanthropy and contribution. Rather, as one respondent argued, altruistic support of the stakes of the Armenian people as such was a universal duty, which was intrinsic to the idea of survival:

> "I think the benevolence towards Armenianness, to maintain Armenianness, is – I believe – strongly developed, because the Armenians feel themselves threatened, well, threatened by extinction. And therefore – as an inherent characteristic - everybody feels obliged, feels responsible for contributing his part, that, what you simply can, so that the culture doesn't disappear."

Making a contribution to the continuance of the Armenian people was thus also an important characteristic – and for most of my informants even a requirement – for being identified as successful *Armenian*. As a concept it did not only concern the economic elite, but every Armenian. With regard to the economic elite, it seemed that the mere accumulation of economic capital, which was not turned into a common good at all, was especially not appreciated.

> "Money, this has got to do little with diaspora and life, with the Armenian life, ok, because I can have all the money in the world, but as an Armenian I have achieved little or nothing, as an Armenian *nota bene*!"

Success and therefore capital had to be shared - even it was not of a monetary kind. Actually, the kind of contribution was supposed to correspond to the individual capabilities.

Also among my informants the feeling of an outstanding guilt or duty towards their people or since recently, the Republic of Armenia, existed. Several Armenians from the Republic felt that their absence from their homeland and their lack of ability to contribute to its prosperity, demanded retribution. One of my informants referred to Raffi Hovannisian[5], the first foreign minister of the Third Republic of Armenia as an example to illustrate his own plans:

> "It is about coming back to the things that again you do or that knowledge you accumulate in outside and you then bring and you pay to your nation. So, he [Raffi Hovannisian] really brings back this knowledge or things he accumulated outside of Armenia. [...] I also like to have a teaching or something in Armenia at the end of my career that would be a great thing which I like to have, when I finish, just to transform or to pay back."

---

[5] Raffi Hovannisian, the son of the American-Armenian Professor Richard Hovannisian emigrated from the USA to the Republic of Armenia after its independence and became its first foreign minister. He was the first of several Diaspora Armenians who – in the aftermath of the independence – came to Armenia to provide help in the process of nation building with their skills (Panossian 1998: 169).

In many cases, smaller or larger acts of contribution were already put into practice or planned by my interviewees like setting up a foundation to render support to Armenia or helping Armenian children by financing their education. On a smaller scale, the idea of contribution as a duty also existed, for example, as one of my interview partners said, many members of the *Kulturverein* were still paying their membership fees even though they actually had left the association.

Whether action was oriented towards the diaspora or the homeland did not necessarily correlate with one's origin. Since the disastrous earthquake in Armenia in 1988, the financial and material support of the homeland had become an "*operative paradigm in the homeland-diaspora relations*" (Panossian 1998: 175, italics by P.). Similar to Schwalgin's observation that the duty to support the homeland had been integrated into the identity concept of Diaspora Armenians (Schwalgin 2004: 115), Armenia also appeared as an important focus of charitable activities among the Diaspora Armenians of my research. As one of my respondents from the Middle East maintained:

> "Of course you can also help Armenia. There is my brother-in-law and others who send medicine to Armenia and support Armenians in ways like that, the hospitals and so on. This is of course also a way to become successful and to become famous."

In contrast to Schwalgin, who identifies this notion of contribution or sacrifice as a key element in a specific diasporic discourse on what it takes to be a "pure" Armenian, which was launched by diaspora elites (Schwalgin&Sökefeld 2000: 4-5), here again the lack of difference between the perceptions and practices of Diaspora Armenians and Republic Armenians - even if they were not involved in the institutionalized diaspora and had lived only for a short time in the diaspora - was striking.

Excursus: Habitus and success

Talking about Armenian values and norms, which are related to success, my informants tended to depict the Armenians as a people with an immanent high esteem for knowledge and education, which stems from their rich cultural legacy. Although, this habitus, which can best be described as "educated middle-class", was in general also ascribed to the population of the Republic of Armenia, it was often denied to the recent immigrants from there. A strong emic differentiation between Diaspora Armenians and Republic Armenian on the basis of geographical origin was already observed in other recent fieldworks of different sites (Schwalgin 2004: 111-118; Tauber 1999: 83f.; Bakalian 1994: 21; Ritter 2007: 37f.; Dahinden 2008: 70f.). Negative ascriptions to Republic Armenians in the different field sites are nearly congruent and culminate in the accusation that they were traitors of the nation (e.g. Bakalian 1994: 21). This is added by the reproach of trading Armenianness for material wellbeing. Ritter quotes a Diaspora Armenian from Boston:

> "Les *Haïastantsi*[6] ont, eux, le choix de venir ici, pas nous [...]. Ils sont en train de brader leur identité contre des supermarchés et des voitures." (ibid. 2007: 37-38; italics by R.)

Ritter describes the social position of the immigrants from the Republic in North America as "un diaspora dans le diaspora" (ibid. 2007: 37). Dahinden and Ishkanian remark as well that Armenians from the Republic in Switzerland and the USA remained at the borders of the already resident communities and hardly benefited from the existent institutional structure (Ishkanian 2002: 386; Dahinden 2008: 71).

Also during my research, several voices from the community charged the recent immigrants with voluntaristic migration, which was not enforced by expulsion, political persecution or other calamities. With regard to their self-concept as a victim diaspora, the migration from the Armenian Republic was not legitimized.

---

[6] Armenian expression for Armenians from the Republic of Armenia.

Besides, the immigration of Armenians from the Republic was said to have led to crime and delinquency in the community, which endangered the good reputation of the Diaspora Armenians in Hamburg (see also Tauber 1999: 86). One respondent commented on the vicious circle of irregular immigration and delinquency and the (initial) distrust which it caused among the Diaspora Armenians:

> "This is really a sad development. This has led to the point that we Diaspora Armenians - let's say - found any Armenian from Armenia guilty as long as his innocence wasn't proven, from the start. Because we – it is a kind of prejudice, but it had developed like this in the meantime – you have heard so many stories from all sides so that you have taken a defensive position, because you were afraid."

Moreover, as Tauber observed, Armenians from the Republic were assumed to have "no sense for the life in the diaspora" (Tauber 1999: 65; translation by C.T.). This view was still held by some.

Nevertheless, as the development in the communal institution suggests, the practical exclusion of the Republic Armenians, which was observed by Tauber, had crumbled in the meantime. These changes seem to correlate with a re-defining and re-drawing of the emic line of exclusion. In contrast to the first years of the immigration influx, it was not simply drawn on the basis of geographical origin. Rather it was based on habitus, i.e. Republic Armenians who did not comply with the general image of an Armenian as it was sketched by my informants were excluded. They were the "Others".

One respondent subsumed the features of the habitus of those "Others" under the Armenian word "rabis" which can be translated as "bumpkin". According to this informant typical rabis shared a low educational background, they preferred a certain haircut, clothing and "language". Thus, they were incompatible with the prototypical "cultivated Armenian" which was appreciated by my informants. Apparently, rabis did not share the Armenian striving for cultural capital and distinction. This deviation was often ascribed to the Soviet socialization these Armenians had experienced. According to my informants – both Republic and Diaspora Armenians – the Armenian system of values had been corrupted by 70 years of Soviet and Russian influence and the deprivations connected with the Communist system. The habitus of the rabis was also associated with the status as asylum seeker. The model of success of those Republic Armenians who sought asylum was distinguished and reduced to the subsistence of their life as well as the public display of the quick and short-lived gain of economic status by big cars, gold, jewelry and other status symbols.

> "[...] I think the Armenians [from the Republic of Armenia] who came as students to Germany are primarily concerned with obtaining an education. This is what they see as success. But others who don't come to Germany for education, but as asylum seekers, I don't know, they have different interests, they have a different understanding of 'success' [...] Armenians who come now, in the first place, I think, they are mostly concerned with their financial covering [...]. Because they probably won't stay in Germany or something like that, they don't have all the possibilities and concentrate primarily on getting a job and then, to get money."

This distinction was not only made by Diaspora Armenians, but also by Armenians from the Armenian Republic.

In fact, the restrictive force of the legal status as an asylum seeker living under the condition of "suspended deportation" (Ger.: *Duldung*) or, worse, illegality and the low socio-economic status, which was due to it, were actually acknowledged as structural obstacles to the appreciated model of success. Anyhow, one Republic Armenian considered it a mere problem of the valid legal provisions, which meant an insurmountable threshold to the immigrants, and not essentially a problem of a different notion of success. He implicated that migration of those Armenians was actually also oriented on social ascent, but the upward mobility of the second generation was impeded by the German immigration policy and the parents' ignorance of the German educational system. From his point of view this was a disaster as in these cases the self-sacrifice which the parents made by migrating and working in low-paid jobs did not result in better opportunities of their offspring.

The relation to the residence society – "Good interference" and reputation

Armenian relations to the non-Armenian environment were located in the tension-filled area between the approval of integration and the fear of assimilation. Especially living in a Christian surrounding, where ethnic boundaries were not upheld by an essential religious difference, was associated with a high risk of losing Armenianness. Notions of integration and assimilation were also discussed in the context of "success" in the community of Hamburg. Several respondents of different origin pointed out that Armenians' success in their respective host countries was dependent on the ability to find balance on the narrow divide between assimilation and integration.

> "[..] the Armenians in the diaspora - they never had a problem with the society they have lived in, because they have always become a part of the society. It is true that maybe they had a different culture sometimes, but they accept the dominant culture that is the majority, and they have integrated themselves, but they have never given up their own identity."

The continuous historical necessity of adaption to non-Armenian environments was expressed in metaphorical sayings like "water always finds a gorge in the rock" or "to go through butter like a hot knife". The term "integration" was connoted with a positive process by which one gained access to cultural resources of the host society:

> "If you don't know your own way, you cannot compare, you cannot discern the advantage and disadvantage of the other. We don't say 'assimilate', that we Armenians get dissolved wholly into German society, but we say '100 per cent integration' – that means: We have our cultural heritage, we have our national, historical, religious and so on feeling, but it doesn't impede our participation in the German culture, in the German wealth of this culture and to develop an appropriate sense of responsibility."

Learning and adopting cultural traits identified as positive and benefiting from the synergy effect of these two "cultures" was welcomed. One Armenian from the Republic of Armenia called it the principle of "good interference". Furthermore, the learning of the language of the host country and multi-lingualism as such were held in high esteem as this was seen as a specific Armenian asset, which, for example, had already distinguished the successful Armenian merchants in the past centuries. Moreover, it was the adoption of certain values and behavioural norms considered as typically German (e.g. punctuality, business culture, debating and conflict culture), which was valued as a gain by some. Finally, the issue of integration seemed to be a question of pragmatism (see also Brednikova et al. 1997: 58f.). However, the other side of the coin of the often-mentioned "flexibility" was the risking of the roots of Armenianness and to fall victim to assimilation.

To what extent my Armenian informants in Hamburg were integrated into the German society cannot be ascertained here. In general informants showed a refined knowledge of German society, medial discourses and political ongoing. In diverse contexts some described themselves as German citizens or as beneficiaries of the German society and accordingly felt responsibility towards it. At the same time a certain practical distance was maintained: Several interviewees emphasized that it was not acceptable for an Armenian to receive, for example, social benefits. One of my informants had even paid back his scholarship, which he once had received from a German institution. This striving for economic autonomy from the host country was seen as an asset, which also distinguished Armenians from other immigrants who had come to Germany in the past decades.

The awareness of the importance of the relation to the host society included a sensitive perception of the society's power of identity ascription (see also Bakalian 1994: 7) and thus the valuation of a good reputation in the major society. Some Armenians - both from the Diaspora as well as the Armenian Republic – mentioned a good reputation as a sign of success of a diaspora community. The Armenian communities in the Middle East were given as an example of successful relations between Armenians and non-Armenians. There, according to my informants, Armenians had earned a good reputation as honest, efficient and trustworthy businessmen, craftsmen, military servants etc. and were met with respect.

6.3 Success as a community in Hamburg

As I already showed in the previous chapters, notions of individual success were often intertwined with the collective, i.e. the Armenian diaspora and the Armenian people respectively. To further discern in which way notions of success manifested themselves on the practical level I examined what success meant in the concrete context of living as a diaspora community in Hamburg. Questions aimed at uncovering the self-perception as a diaspora community as well as the specific goals this community had set itself in order to be successful. While notions of success turned out to be rather consensual, only differing in finer details, concrete community goals, which were considered important to reach, were more heterogeneous.

Self-perception as a diaspora community in Hamburg and Germany

The preponderant view on the local community in Hamburg and the diaspora in Germany as such was oscillating between critical but hopeful, and disappointed and fatalistic. The most positive evaluation described the recent development as a "renaissance" of the diaspora in Germany. This opinion was uttered by an informant who was active in the current national and trans-/international networking and interaction of Armenian institutions. However, no one was willing to label the diaspora "successful". This was especially due to the low degree of development of diasporic structures in Hamburg and Germany. As a root cause for this underdevelopment, the specific historical and societal context of Germany was identified, which had led to a hesitant establishment of the Armenians of the first immigration waves and which had impeded the installation of a solid communal infrastructure. The Republic Armenians constituted the first immigration wave, which was not based on sojourning and promised a growing numerical stability and coherence. Apart from this historical and political background, the contextual factors of the residence in Germany were perceived differently: On the one hand the liberal Christian society seemed to open the door to assimilation; on the other, cultural pluralism warranted an undisturbed community life and offered the opportunity of cultural expression in the public sphere, potentially, for example, in the form of the building of religious edifices.

Internal conflicts, absorption of new members and financial instability had been consuming the community's resources in the last forty years. Problems that were further perceived to distract the community were: Suboptimal cohesion of the Armenians and their organizations, lack of institutional and communal stability caused by high fluctuation of migrants, a low level of cultural life, the lack of spatial concentration (in Hamburg as well as in Germany in general), high internal heterogeneity regarding origin and, thus, difference in cultural backgrounds. The existing organizational infrastructure – here, in the shape of the Kulturverein in Hamburg - was especially criticized by Armenians originating from diaspora settlements in the Middle East, where a strong institutional framework was taken for granted. From their point of view, the association did not yet fulfill its classical role as a communal institution in the diaspora. One respondent from the Middle East claimed:

> "Well, [...] if for example we look at the clubs, which we have here, [...]: Many people don't go to the clubs, it is just people who have problems who go

there. One needs a visa, another needs something else [...]. This atmosphere of normal clubs as we know them, where you go to eat, to play music and then you celebrate and so on: It is not that optimal yet. That means there is still a lack of homogeneity. If homogeneity was given then you would see this in the clubs, [in] events of artistic character and so on. Now they sometimes have something like that, but it is not steady. These are always activities by some individuals who try to get someone, a singer and so on. They are all very nice and beautiful, but it is not steady yet and it is not of a high level. It is always spontaneous, the whole thing. It is not organized yet. Of course we have a community, but [...] what you need is also a real church, a real club."

As my informant put it the association neither provided a space for the constitution of the social unity nor did it offer opportunities for the maintenance and reproduction of what he perceived as Armenian culture on a "high level". Besides, the respondent mentioned the importance of a "real church" for the community – an opinion which could be found among almost all Armenians I interviewed. The lack of a church as an institution and as a physical place was associated with different communal shortcomings, which I will illustrate a little later.

Armenian diasporas perceived as successful were the communities in the USA and France as well as the communities in the Middle East, even though in different ways: The mentioned communities in the Western hemisphere were marked by their political strength and activity, for example in terms of lobbying for the recognition of the genocide. In contrast, the diaspora communities in the Middle East were considered particularly successful in the issue of guarding "Armenianness". In contrast, the Russian diaspora, which was growing in influence, was not mentioned at all. Non-Armenian diasporas, which served for comparison in success, were the Jewish and the Turkish diasporas. The Turkish diaspora did not embody an adaptable success model, but it was perceived as "successful" regarding its influence on German politics by their lobby organizations as well as by naturalized Turkish individuals who were members of German political parties. This diasporic power was ascribed to the quantity of Turks in Germany, which allegedly easily enabled them to reach a critical mass for diasporic agency. In contrast, the Jewish diaspora was cited as a success model on terms of similarity. This was due to perceived parallels with regard to origin, fate, size and structure of the diaspora. Albeit, none of my respondents saw the Armenian diaspora as being on the same level as the Jewish one; as one of them formulated it, the Armenians were "light years away" from being as successful as the Jews. Admirable achievements of Jewish diaspora included successful diasporic cohesion and internal organization as well as the high rate of successful individuals, the latter phenomenon being ascribed to the Jewish way of upbringing.

Goals as a diaspora community

Concrete goals of the diaspora were mostly formulated by Armenians who were involved in diasporic work. Most of these ideas have to be read as opinions of individuals first as I cannot say to what extent they are consensual in the community. For one of my interviewees who was involved in diaspora activities, the strengthening and reproduction of the community as a diaspora community was a major concern. This demanded the ensuring of the reproduction of cultural Armenianness:

> "[...] well, it would be a success if I saw that the next generation was at least on the same level regarding Armenian identity [...] as my generation, at least."

As about half of the community members were from the Republic of Armenia, it also meant to tackle the issue of their integration and to foster the "return" of the deviant ones to the Armenian community and Armenian. However, the sustenance of Armenianness was not only a question of the local promotion of Armenian tradition, values, norms and community life, but also a question of creating a diaspora elite, which once would be able to stabilize the community financially e.g. by donations. In this Armenian elite economic striving and awareness of Armenian identity ideally merged:

> "In order to donate money you first have to have money. Hence we have to try to push as many members of our own community to the top as possible, that means to support [them], so that they become successful and at the same time – and this is the important thing and the reason why success alone is not enough – these Armenians have to identify themselves with the cause, they have to deal with their identity [...] That means, both have to exist: The interest in keeping one's own identity, to pass it on and to keep being active in this field and, secondly, being successful as a person, as an individual. Only when these two features come together, it works out."

A similar point mentioned by several respondents was the social mobility of the diaspora members. Social mobility was also seen as an important factor with regard to the potential and agency of the community, and as a feature which the community in Hamburg still lacked. In this respect, France was often put forward as an example where the Armenian diaspora was successfully established inside the host society. There, the Armenians were said to have penetrated all levels of the socio-economic strata, were well-integrated into the French society and political life and enjoyed a good reputation.

With regard to political participation, one goal was the strengthening of the Armenian lobby. One of my informants maintained that with regard to lobbying the recognition of the genocide was currently the most important goal but not the only one. Also, the lobbying for projects in Armenia was a possible field of future political activity. The entering of official German politics and institutions by party membership as it was practiced by the Turks in Germany and Armenians in Lebanon, Iran, but also France and USA (see Tölölyan 2000: 126) was thought of as difficult by the above-cited informant on the grounds of the demographic weakness of the Armenian diaspora: Until now, the diaspora had been too much in flux and weak in numbers and the newly arrived generation of Republic Armenians was still too busy with establishing themselves to provide personalities who were able – also by naturalization – to join the formal German political arena.

Some of my respondents from the New Diaspora doubted whether the focusing on the recognition of the genocide served the interests of the Armenians in the diaspora. Though they shared the opinion that the genocide had to be recognized, they voiced their concern that the promotion of this topic as the sole Armenian cause confirmed an image of the Armenians in their host societies as victims and inferiors and thus concealed the positive aspects of Armenians and their culture:

> I1: "[...] the genocide is really an important issue for us, but we have the impression that we are only known in the world in the context of the genocide topic. But we have other, so many, thousand rich cultures and other distinct events of success, which are actually never emphasised. And then when we appear somewhere [...] then we are pitied by someone. And this annoys you sometimes [...] because you are a competitive person, you are actually as good as the others, and then you don't need to be welcomed by someone: 'Bummer! They have had the genocide, let us support them' [...] It's a pity and then we are backing the striving for recognition, but we also try to show from other angles that we are successful in the present world, but that we have also been in thousands years of civilisation."
> I2: "And you shouldn't reduce yourself to that. I am of the opinion that the whole culture with regard to..."
> I1: "...to see it as a renaissance"

It remained unclear whether this longing for an alternative or "additional" image as a "success diaspora" correlated with belonging to the Old Diaspora and New Diaspora respectively or whether it was dependent on other factors.

Roots and trunk – The necessity of building a church

Among the institutions, which accompanied and organized transnational and local Armenian life throughout its diasporic history, the Armenian Apostolic Church –

founded in 301 AD - showed to be the most consistent and most important one (Aghanian 2007: 15). From the 14th century onwards, the Church not only occupied the role of the spiritual institution but also developed into the pre-eminent and singular political leader of the community. In the 19th century its political dominance was challenged by the appearance of the Diaspora parties, which were based on a nationalistic and rather anti-clerical ideology (Tölölyan 1988: 57). Nonetheless, the Church's role was not restricted to a mere religious function. Rather, it was of fundamental importance to community building. As Bakalian points out with regard to the Armenian communities in USA:

> "Communal life became organized around the churches. Immigrants would congregate in rented meeting halls or church buildings, but as soon as they had sufficient funds, they would buy or build their own edifices. These houses of worship doubled as locales for social gatherings; almost invariably, they were comprised of a sanctuary and a large hall (and a kitchen) that became the hub of a burgeoning collective existence. Where there was a church there was also politics." (Bakalian 1994: 89)

It can be seen also in this context that the situation of the Armenian community in Hamburg, which was marked by institutional instability, was deplored, while the community in Cologne was perceived as the centre of the Armenian diaspora in Germany by some interviewees. This community, which was largely constituted by Turkish Armenians, harboured the Armenian Apostolic Diocese and was in possession of a church building of their own: the church *Surb Sahak-Mesrop*. Though the community of Hamburg was able to use the church of St. Gertrud for religious celebrations, the lack of a church of their own was perceived as the reason for the communal weakness[1]. One Diaspora Armenian stated:

---

[1] It must be mentioned that these statements were not delivered by Turkish Armenians who are said to prioritise the Church as an institution of Armenianness (Tauber 1999: 80), but by interviewees from the Middle East and Armenia. Especially the emphasis of the Church's role by the Republic Armenians is worth mentioning as the religious life had been restricted in the Socialist Republic of Armenia, which, for example, had resulted in the fact that many Republic Armenians had not even

> "It is not by coincidence that the community in Germany is not as strong as other communities. Of course, we have not started at the bottom, we have started with the leaves on the top and those fall down. You have to have a trunk. The church has always been a root, a trunk. Everything has developed out of it. In [my home country] it was the same, many different schools evolved from it and so on. But in the beginning there was a church [...]."

The church in its nuclear role as founder of communal relations was not replaceable, even as modes of everyday communication and opportunities for *Vergemeinschaftung* changed with the time, for example, by the internet. It was also a general opinion that the observance or practice of religiosity was not the central concern. Rather it was maintained that the Armenians attended church chiefly on the important Christian holidays – Christmas and Easter. Although religiosity decreased, as one informant from the Middle East stated, it was expected that the Church would still be respected as an important social institution by the future generations:

> "[...] the new generation will probably change with time. I mean religiosity in general in the societies [will change], when the young generation is not that religious any more. But they respect that and go to church – sometimes, because it has to be like that (laughs)."

The church was associated with the genuine place of Armenian gathering, which was crucial for the establishment and keeping of intra-ethnic social contacts and relations. At least on Sundays, as one Republican Armenian put it, Armenians would "see each other" and thus have a stable space for social interaction, "otherwise they are some sort of spread everywhere". For church services, another Republic Armenian informant stated, all Armenians would "come out of their cor-

---

been baptised. This was also reason why one Turkish Armenian respondent once questioned the Armenianness of such Republican Armenians. But the importance of the Church was not just a lip service for the latter as at least two of my interviewees from Armenia attended church services when time allowed for it.

ners". The social character and importance of Armenian Church services was conveyed to me when I attended the Christmas mass on 6th January. While the bishop, accompanied by a small choir in the front, was conducting the liturgy, the congregation was chatting and turning heads as often as new visitors entered the church. During mass there was a steady movement of people in and out of the church, having talks outdoors and re-entering again. According to my estimation Christmas service was attended by about 150 to 200 people. That was still only a rather small percentage of the total Armenian population in Hamburg, but far more than at the events in the Kulturverein. Thus, the church seemed to be an alternative Armenian meeting place for those who otherwise had no time or were not interested in participating in associational life.

My informants also used to point to the historical role of the church to establish the cohesion, reproduce cultural identity and impede assimilation. Even if the Armenians had lost their identification by cultural practice and language – like the Armenians in the USA were said to have done – they would still turn out in masses to the church once or twice a year:

> "[the Armenians in Glendale] have big churches and so on. There they told me: When it is Easter it is so full that the fire brigade comes and tries to hinder the people with water [from entering] (both laugh), there are thousands! But only [...] one, two times a year."

The church thus was the harbour of the community to which, it was said, the young people would return to let their children become christened even if they themselves had not shown any interest in Armenianness or the Armenian Church before.

Several informants also maintained that the presence of a church of their own would have a soothing effect on the social and inner integration problems of the Armenian community – especially with regard to the issue of Republic Armenians, who were often perceived as disintegrated and oriented towards the Russians.

The church as a physical and social institution, as some of my interviewees hoped, would render a new self-confidence and identification as Armenians and, thus, give orientation to those Armenian immigrants from Armenia who were perceived as deviant. Also, Armenian activity was hoped to be raised, as soon as a church building would centralize the otherwise spread Armenians. Nevertheless, the future of the project was not foreseeable: Ten months after the first call for donations the community had collected almost 6000€. Without the financial commitment of the wealthy individuals or Armenian institutions, the dream of a communal church would probably not come true.

7 Conclusion

This research has given a manifold insight of the relation of diaspora and success as well as the historical and recent development of the Armenian diaspora. It showed that the Armenian diaspora exceeds the historical Armenian statehood in continuity and has developed an institutional structure of its own, which, until these days, serves the maintenance and further development as a diasporic nation. Though the coercive character of life in the diaspora being a people without an independent state vanished with the establishment of the Third Republic of Armenia in 1991, the diasporic situation is re-interpreted as a structural advantage of Armenia, thus leading to an acceptance of the permanent existence of the diaspora. Furthermore, it looks back on a long existence as a victim, but also as a successful trade and middleman diaspora, while these characteristics tend to be intermingled. In contrast to other migrant communities, Armenian communities are also today rather perceived as an economically successful "middle class" or even "upper class" minority in their host societies.

In contrast to other Armenian communities of recent date e.g. in the Middle East, the USA and France, which were major destinations of Armenian migration in the aftermath of the genocide from Turkey, the diaspora in Germany had been essentially nurtured by Armenian immigrations from diverse countries of the Middle East since the 1960s and has not had the chance to solidify its organizational structure due to fluctuation. The early prevalent sojourner mentality only changed recently with the numerous arrivals of Republic Armenians. Although their definite continuance is threatened by the restrictive provisions of German migration policy, the Republic Armenians probably can be seen as a positive potential for stabilization and the further development of the Armenian diaspora in Germany. Whether the diaspora is successful in socio-economic terms, as it is stated for other post-genocide diasporas in the USA, France and Lebanon, cannot be ascertained here.

Finally, until today the Armenians constitute a "hidden minority" in Germany, being hardly visible in the public sphere, though a change towards a more offensive external self-presentation seems to be taking place. While the diaspora had been muted for the first decades by the presence of the politically potent and huge Turkish migrant community, recent events bear witness of a new political self-consciousness in Germany's public space regarding e.g. their primary political aim, the recognition of the Armenian genocide. In this context, relations to the majority society in terms of involving German prominent personalities as a mouthpiece appear to be a strategy to gain power in an unequal game. At the same time, the augmented activity of classical transnationally operating diasporic organizations in the diaspora in Germany such as the Diocese of the Armenian Apostolic Church in 1992, the appearance of branches of rivaling Diaspora parties Dashnakzutyun and the Ramgavar and their respective affiliate social organizations and the philanthropic institutions in the last ten years point to a growing transnationalization of the German diaspora, which until then – regarding its organizational structure – was primarily concerned with cultural sustenance in the localities. While during my research most Armenians evaluated the Armenian diaspora in Germany as unsuccessful, a minority of translocally and transnationally operating diasporic actors judged the recent situation as the dawn of a renaissance of Armenians in Europe and Germany. Furthermore, the recent initiatives on building or purchasing churches in Hanau, Hamburg and Berlin – whether they will be successful or not – may indicate that the communities were finally recognizing the permanence of their stay in Germany.

Regarding the spatial distribution of communities in Germany, the community of Hamburg is rather located at the rim of the Armenian diaspora, distant from the agglomerations in the southern and western region of Germany. Organizationally, it was mainly connected to the nation-wide Armenian diaspora by its membership in the umbrella organization Zentralrat der Armenier in Deutschland. The community can be described as multi-layered, being shaped by multiple waves of migration from diverse countries. The first community at the beginning of the 20th century had had the character of a trade diaspora; migration then was attracted due to Hamburg's character as a port city and, therefore, commercial centre. Today, this perception of Hamburg has almost vanished. For most of my interviewees, Hamburg did not bear a special meaning as destination of migration. Furthermore, international trade played a minor role in the Armenian community. A growing rate and esteem of self-employment was detectable, but due to the heterogeneous character of the community after several waves of migrations and its lack of consolidation this was hard to determine. At the same time economic (success) strategies seemingly did not rely on ethnic enclavement or the realization of ethnic economic niches. In comparison to other migrant groups Armenians were hard to discover in urban space – culturally as well as economically and politically.

After about 40 years of institutionalization the community in Hamburg was equipped with three registered organizations of which two were visibly acting as communal associations. While associational fragmentation was, thus, rather low, the institutionalized community had been internally split according to geographical origins almost from the start. However, those internal boundaries shifted during time. In the last 15 years, the boundary was roughly drawn between Diaspora Armenians and Republic Armenians. The Republic Armenians who had been excluded during the 1990s - charged, among others, of being fatally ignorant of life in the diaspora and traitors of the Armenian nation - now made up a high proportion of the users of the main institutions and were also present in the steering committees. Though this amalgamation was still not free of conflict, the revitalizing power of this immigration wave displayed itself in the augmented import of producers of "original" Armenian culture from Armenia. Still, the self-perception of the community's success was rather negative as structures were felt to be not solid and little developed due to diverse reasons, among them, cultural heterogeneity, lack of financial backing as well as the lack of a the central institution in Armenian communities: a church of one's own. The latter was perceived as a necessity for achieving a greater cohesion among the Armenians in Hamburg and building a church was thus a concrete project of the community.

The local project of building a church was seemingly not supported by the economic elite of the Armenians. This lack of support was one hint for a phenomenon which was mentioned during my research: That the well-off diasporists of the region were not soothing the financial needs of the local structures. Seemingly economic wealth did not necessarily correlate with local diasporic commitment. This observation further opens up the question whether - and if, in what way economic success is connected to a certain degree of independence from the local community structures and local intra-ethnic relations.

Furthermore, the project of building a church can be interpreted as a decision to end the idea of sojourning and to establish oneself in Hamburg. This was also reflected in the external presentation of the Armenian institutionalized community: The interest in rooting Armenians visibly in the German society and its public space became obvious in the perception of the Armenian stone cross monument in Bremen. Secondly, it implied that an awakening of identity politics had taken place, which comprised the confrontation of the German public and the Turkish community with the Armenian genocide and, thus, the establishment as a recognized historical victim of the Ottoman Empire. Nevertheless, the establishment of the Armenians as a victim diaspora was not a consensual or at least the only goal as several Armenians preferred to be perceived as members of a "success" diaspora, which was associated with cultural richness and superb educational level. This latter self-image is reflected in the Armenian concept of success, which was displayed by most of my informants.

The Armenian concept of success was embedded in a diasporic discourse on "survival", which was nourished by Armenian history and especially by the experience of the genocide in 1915/16 at the hands of the Turks. The common consciousness of my informants was built on the topos of being a "persecuted or mobile minority under alien rule", which has to overcome the structural disadvantage of this state by exceptional achievements. Thus, the ideal Armenian was described as a "fighter", who – on his own and by his strong work ethic – would push through any kind of hardship. This image was embodied by several Armenians of prominence and was also included in the narratives of life stories.

With regard to the concept of success a dichotomy, between the Armenian family and the Armenian nation turned out to be of importance: While the Armenian nation as a collective was an important point of reference to legitimize success, the family was the most important place of generating success. The family mobilized all its strength to promote the achievements of its offspring - and reap the fruits of prestige -, but the success of the individual had to trickle down on the collective and, for example, nurture the ascent of the next elite in order to be finally recognized. This reinvestment into the Armenian nation, which was called “sacrifice” in discourse, concerned especially economically powerful Armenians, but also every Armenian with regard to his or her individual assets that he or she could share. The logic of this notion is best described with a “chain”, which powers the Armenian survival. A main characteristic of the cultural concept of success is therefore the duty to *share success* with one’s co-ethnics and one’s ethnic collective. In reality, it was not consensual how or what to share as the latent conflict over investment into local versus greater diaspora projects implied. Contrary to the perception of Diaspora Armenians and the literature, I could show in my research that this cultural concept is not bound to a long-endured physical and mental experience of diasporic life, but that it is internalized in detail and practiced by the allegedly sedentary Armenians from the Republic who migrated recently. The recognition of this fact was also reflected in the shifting of emic differentiation from the basis of geographical origin to a certain habitus, which excluded allegedly uncivilized and materially oriented Republic Armenians with insecure status of residence, and thus included the “educated” Republic Armenians into the diasporic in-group.

With regard to the cultural concept of success, I illustrated the importance of cultural capital and how it was generated and further consciously passed on in the familial sphere. Cultural capital was not only appreciated in terms of formal education as “light baggage” under conditions of diasporic mobility, but also as a means of social distinction and, thus, as part of a certain habitus, which indicates the adherence to a certain social class. The habitus of the "diasporic Armenian" can best be described as "educated middle-class". This self-perception was emphasized by the exclusion of those Republic Armenians from the diasporic project who did not display this habitus and were said to be corrupted by their Russian legacy. Cultural capital of the offspring was important also as symbolic capital to the whole family and was displayed in the Armenian social sphere in the form of presentation of cultural skills. With regard to acquisition of this habitus, the family played an immense role as place of inheritance of knowledge and education. The improvement of educational opportunities of the offspring was an important family goal, which was enabled by "sacrifices" made by parents. I discerned that these sacrifices were compensated by the offspring's achievement orientation and that these components built a generation contract. This was especially valid for the relationship between father and male descendants. The orientation in the offspring's future as compensation for present toils indicates an acceptance of delayed gratification by the parents.

Further investigation on social capital indicated that the family was a highly valued social unit. Relations with extra-familial Armenians and non-Armenians each seemed to have their specific place. In the economic realm, intra-ethnic relations apparently were mostly acceptable as vertical or asymmetrical relations, e.g. employer and employee or between businessman and client. Horizontal partnership relations were rather contracted with non-Armenians. My hypothesis is that this was, among others, due to the multiplication of capital by social relations: Business partnership with a German who knows the German market and bureaucratic procedures and regulations and, thus, was in possession of capital (here explicitly mentioned: cultural capital), which was otherwise short due to the migration situation. Moreover, co-ethnic horizontal partnerships in business were perceived as very competitive, which also corresponds to the Armenian notion of successful individuals as lonesome, individualistic fighters. The prevalence of vertical intra-ethnic relations was also mirrored and appreciated in the principle of elite promotion - whether it was based on an institutionalized system, e.g. scholarships by a philanthropic foundation or on personal contacts between a patron and a student. Furthermore, economic strategies showed that the local Armenian community was not perceived as a potential economic resource in terms of "ethnic consumerism" – a fact that was reasoned, among others, with the pettiness of such business. Economic independence was not only sought in the intra-ethnic realm, but also in the relation to the residence society, as, for example, social benefits were refused.

Cultural permeability, open-mindedness towards cooperation with non-Armenians or even striving for positive relations with members of the residence society was also rooted in the notion of integration. Although the risky lurching between integration and assimilation was perceived as endangering Armenian survival, integration and cultural flexibility was seen as an asset, which was traced back to successful Armenians in the past. Integration meant adaptation of positive traits of the alien cultural surrounding and learning of language (i.e. accumulating cultural capital of the foreign society) as well as promoting positive social relations to members of the host society and, thus, gaining symbolic capital as a group. Fear of losing symbolic capital in the residence society was also part of the skepticism towards the migration from the Republic of Armenia as those Armenians were perceived as cultural "Others" who did not strive for the same social distinction. Good social relations to non-Armenians were also important in the context of identity politics where representatives of the host society acted as advocates of the causes of the community.

With regard to economic capital it became clear that it was also not appreciated as a value *per se*. The accumulation of economic wealth was not discouraged at all, but it brought with it the duty to share it with the "nation". Thus, accumulated wealth was often transformed in some kind of public good, a way, which, according to Bourdieu, creates symbolic capital and justifies the elite status in the face of the non-privileged public. In this respect the founding of philanthropic organizations or funds seemed to be a very popular and publicly appreciated strategy among Armenians who could afford it.

8 Epilogue

In this explorative research it could not be clarified to what extent Armenians are perceived and recognized as successful by the majority society in Germany and whether their cultural concept of success pays off in general. Nevertheless, to make a final recourse to the here non-determinable problem of accessibility of the German "market" and the convertibility of foreign cultural capital I want to mention a conversation with an Armenian girl.

One of my Armenian acquaintances had just graduated from school - a "Gymnasium", which was primarily attended by wealthy and white German kids .She planned to study at university. With regard to the imperative of the accumulation of cultural capital she was a true "Armenian": She had achieved excellent grades (being, for example, the best in her German language class), won several local competitions regarding educational achievements (e.g. in language and mathematics). Additionally, she had a talent in fine arts. At the same time her outward appearance conformed to a style, which could mostly be associated with hip hop culture, which was then especially appropriated by the "marginalized", e.g. the non-German youth. She mentioned that her schoolmates categorized her either as a "geek" or as "scum". Those who discriminated against her displayed their socio-economic background with posh clothes, but were inferior regarding their cultural capital, especially due to their relative lack of sophistication in the German language. She felt that she was always perceived by her German schoolmates as the "girl with the black hair" - implicating the racist undertone of the exclusion. Though she exceeded her schoolmates at least in cultural capital, she was refused access to their cliques by her habitus in terms of appearance and taste and by far more determinant her specific "capital" of "not being German".

With this final anecdote I want to hint at the difficulties in assessing the real effecttive power of different forms of capitals and the impact of power holders who can arbitrarily set the rules of access, and the vulnerability that accompanies the diasporic situation.

9 Literature cited

Abrahamian, Levon (2006) *Armenian identity in a changing world.* Mazda Publishers: Costa Mesa, CA.

Adams, Richard (2003) 'International migrations, remittances and the brain drain: A study of 24 labor-exporting countries'. World Bank Policy Research Working Paper #3069 (June).

Aghanian, Denise (2007) *The Armenian Diaspora. Cohesion and fracture.* University Press of America: Lanham, Boulder, New York, Toronto, Plymouth (UK).

Akyol, Cigdem (23.01.2008) 'Ermordeter Journalist Hrant Dink. Schuld ohne Sühne'. Die tageszeitung – TAZ: http://www.taz.de/nc/1/politik/europa/artikel /1/schuld-ohne-suehne&src=PR [April 25 2008].

Armenia Diaspora Conference (no year) 'Population'. http://www.armenia diaspora.com [July 20 2007].

Armenian National Institute – ANI (2008 a) 'Memorial in Braunschweig, Germany'. http://www.armenian-genocide.org/Memorial.152/current_category.64/ memorials_detail.html [June 13 2008].

Armenian National Institute – ANI (2008 b) 'Memorial in Stuttgart, Germany'. http://www.armenian-genocide.org/Memorial.87/current_category.64/memorials _detail.html [June 13 2008].

Armenien.de – Aktuelle Informationen für Armenier und Deutsche in deutscher Sprache (12.04.2007) 'Institutionen. Vereine&Verbände in Deutschland'. http://www.armenien.de/institutionen2.htm [May 14 2007].

Armenier in RheinMain (2008) 'Kirchenbauprojekt Hanau'. http://armenier-rheinmain.de [July 7 2008].

Armenische Kirchen- und Kulturgemeinde Berlin e.V. (28.11.2006) 'Kirchenkauf. Spendensammlung für Kirchenkauf in Berlin'. http://www.armenier-berlin.de [November 10 2009].

Armenischer Kulturverein zu Hamburg e.V. (no year a) [No title]. http://www.armenier-hamburg.de [May 25 2008].

Armenischer Kulturverein zu Hamburg e.V. (no year b) 'Armenische Kirche in Hamburg'. http://www.armenier-hamburg.de/jv/index.php?option=com _content &task=section&id=8&Itemid=29 [June 15 2008].

Armenischer Jugendverband Kilikia e.V. (no year a) [No title]. http://www.armenier-hamburg.de/kilikia [June 15 2008].

Armenischer Jugendverband Kilikia e.V. (no year b) 'Satzung'. http://www.armenier-hamburg.de/kilikia/index.php?option=com_content&task= view&id=12&Itemid=51 [June 15 2008].

Armenischer Jugendverband Kilikia e.V. (no year c) 'Über uns'. http://www.armenier-hamburg.de/kilikia/ueber-uns [September 15 2011].

Aslanian, Sebouh (2004) 'Trade diaspora versus colonial state: Armenian merchants, the English East India Company, and the High Court of Admirality in London, 1748-1752'. Diaspora. 13 (1): 37-100.

Aufenthaltsgesetz – AufenthG (2008) 'Gesetz über den Aufenthalt, die Erwerbstätigkeit und die Integration von Ausländern im Bundesgebiet'. Aufenthaltsgesetz in der Fassung der Bekanntmachung vom 25. Februar 2008 (BGBl. I S. 162), zuletzt geändert durch Artikel 2 Abs. 3 des Gesetzes vom 13. März 2008 (BGBl. I S. 313). Stand: Neugefasst durch Bek. v. 25.2.2008 I 162. Zuletzt geändert durch Art. 2 Abs. 3 G v. 13.3.2008 I 313.

Avagian, Grigor (1994) *Armenia and Armenians in the world*. Omega-N: Yerevan.

Bade, Klaus J.; Oltmer, Jochen (2004) *Normalfall Migration*. Bundeszentrale für politische Bildung: Bonn.

Bakalian, Anny (1994) *Armenian-Americans. From being to feeling Armenian*. Transaction Publishers: New Brunswick, New York.

Baladouni, Vahé (1998) 'Introduction'. In: Baladouni, Vahé; Makepeace, Margaret (eds.) *Armenian merchants of the seventeenth and eighteenth centuries. English East India Company sources*. American Philosophical Society: Philadelphia: XV-XXXVII.

Basu, Anuradha (2006) 'Ethnic minority entrepreneurship'. In: Casson, Marc; Yeung, Bernard; Basu, Anuradha; Wadeson, Nigel (eds.) *The Oxford Handbook of Entrepreneurship*. Oxford University Press: Oxford, New York et al.: 580-600.

Bernard, H. Russel (2002) *Research methods in anthropology. Qualitative and quantitative approaches*. Altamira Press: Walnut Creek, Lanham, New York, Oxford, third edition.

Bonacich, Edna (1973) 'A theory of middleman minorities'. American Sociological Review. 38 (5): 583-594.

Boudjikanian, Aïda K. (1988) 'Les Arméniens du Moyen-Orient. Leur existence actuelle à la lumière du passé récent'. Les Temps Modernes. 43 (504-506): 235-257.

Bourdieu, Pierre (1982) *Die feinen Unterschiede. Kritik der gesellschaftlichen Urteilskraft*. Suhrkamp Verlag: Frankfurt a.M..

Bourdieu, Pierre (1985) *Sozialer Raum und „Klassen". Leçon sur la leçon. Zwei Vorlesungen*. Suhrkamp Verlag: Frankfurt a.M, 1st edition.

Bourdieu, Pierre (1987) *Sozialer Sinn. Kritik der theoretischen Vernunft*. Suhrkamp: Frankfurt a.M.

Bourdieu, Pierre (2005) *Die verborgenen Mechanismen der Macht*. VSA-Verlag: Hamburg.

Bourdieu, Pierre; Wacquant, Loïc J. D. (1996) *Reflexive Anthropologie*. Suhrkamp: Frankfurt a.M.

Brednikova, Ol'ga; Čikadze, Elena; Snisarenko, Anatolij (1997) 'Armenisches Leben in St. Petersburg. Entstehung und Entwicklung einer armenischen Diaspora-Gemeinde'. In: Oswald, Ingrid; Viktor Voronkov (eds.) *Post-sowjetische Ethnizitäten. Ethnische Gemeinden in St. Petersburg und Berlin/Potsdam*. Berliner Debatte Wissenschaftsverlag: Berlin: 55-73.

Bundesamt für Migration und Flüchtlinge (2006) 'Migration, Integration und Asyl in Zahlen'. http://www.bamf.de/cln_011/nn_443728/SharedDocs/Anlagen /DE/DasBAMF/Publikationen/broschuere-statistik-2005.html [July 14 2008].

Bundesamt für Migration und Flüchtlinge (2007) 'Minas. Atlas über Migration, Integration und Asyl'. http://www.bamf.de/cln_011/nn_441806/Shared

Docs/Anlagen/DE/Integration/Publikationen/Sonstige/atlas-minaspublikation.html?_nnn=true [July 14 2008].

Christopher, Andrew Mark (1975) 'Armenians in cities'. The Armenian Review. 28 (3-111): 272-282.

Cohen, Abner (1971) 'Cultural strategies in the organization of trading diasporas'. In: Meillasoux, Claude (ed.) *The development of indigenous trade and markets in West Afrika*. Oxford University Press: London et al.: 266-281.

Cohen, Robin (1997) *Global diasporas. An introduction*. UCL Press: London.

Dabag, Mihran (1994) 'Armenier in Deutschland'. In: Berliner Institut für Vergleichende Sozialforschung (ed.) *Ethnische Minderheiten in Deutschland*. Edition Parabolis: Berlin, second delivery, chapter 3.2.5: 1-14.

Dabag, Mihran (1995) 'Die armenische Minderheit'. In: Schmalz-Jacobsen, Cornelia; Hansen, Georg (eds.) *Ethnische Minderheiten in der Bundesrepublik Deutschland*. Beck: München: 61-72.

Dahinden, Janine (2008) 'Deconstructing mythological foundations of ethnic identities and ethnic group formation: Alban-speaking and new Armenian Immigrants in Switzerland'. Journal for Ethnic and Migration Studies. 34 (1): 55-76.

Dekmejian, R. Hrair (1997) 'The Armenian Diaspora'. In: Hovannisian, Richard G. (ed.) *The Armenian people from ancient to modern times. Volume II*. Macmillan Press LTD: Houndmills, Basingstoke, Hampshire, London: 413-443.

Diözese der Armenischen Kirche in Deutschland (1998) ‚Kurzinformation zu Geschichte und Gegenwart der Armenisch- Apostolischen Orthodoxen Kirche'. Köln.

Evangelische Kirche in Deutschland (16.06.2005) 'Bundestag verurteilt Völkermord an den Armeniern. http://www.ekd.de/aktuell_presse/news_2005_06_16_2_bundestag_armenier.html [November 9 2009].

FAZ.NET – Frankfurter Allgemeine Zeitung (25.01.2005) '„Geschichtsfälschung wie in der DDR“'. http://www.faz.net/s/RubCC21B04EE95145B3AC877C874FB1B611/Doc~E17597BDEB1C44B9EAE46946D16CA7545~ATpl~Ecommon~Scontent.html [May 15 2008].

Fundação Calouste Gulbenkian (2008) 'Activities and grants. Armenian communities'. http://www.gulbenkian.pt/index.php?section=24 [July 7 2008].

Gesellschaft für bedrohte Völker (20.04.2005) 'Armenian-Diskussion am 21. April 2005 im Bundestag – Völkermord anerkennen!'. http://www.gfbv.de/presse mitphp?id=138&stayInsideTree=1 [June 30 2009].

Glick-Schiller, Nina; Basch, Linda Basch; Szanton Blanc, Cristina (1995) 'From immigrant to transmigrant: Theorizing transnational migration'. Anthropological Quarterly. 68 (1): 48-63.

Gray, Ann (2007) *Research practice for cultural studies.* Sage Publications: Los Angeles, London, New Delhi, Singapore, 5th edition.

Grünberg, Wolfgang; Slabaugh, Dennis L.; Meister-Karanikas, Ralf (1994) *Lexikon der Hamburger Religionsgemeinschaften. Religionsvielfalt der Stadt von A-Z.* Dölling und Galitz Verlag: Hamburg.

Grüne Alternative Liste – GAL (17.01.2008) 'Arme Stadtteile profitieren nicht vom Aufschwung'. http://www.gal-fraktion.de/cms/presse/dok/215/215601.html [June 15 2008].

HAIK – Deutsch Armenischer Studentenclub (2008) 'Eröffnung des AGBU-HAIK Office Germany im Herzen von Frankfurt'. http://www.haiknet.de [July 14 2008].

Hamburger Melderegister (no year a) 'Ausländische Bevölkerung in Hamburg nach Stadtteilen, Familienstand und ausgewählten Staatsangehörigkeiten zum 31.12.2004'. Unpublished extract. Hamburg.

Hamburger Melderegister (no year b) 'Anzahl der Armenier in Hamburg 31.12.1997-31.12.2007'. Unpublished extract. Hamburg.

Harutunian, Martun (2002/2003) 'Ausgewählte Aspekte der Entstehung und Entwicklung armenischer Gemeinschaften in Deutschland'. ISB-Jahrbuch: http://www.isb-bln.de/jahrbuecher/jahrbuch2003/1908.html [April 11 2007].

"Hayastan" All-Armenian Fund (05.11.2007) '„Hayastan" All-Armenian Fund. Nach 15 Jahren weiterhin eine Notwendigkeit?'. Brochure. Poing.

Hirschberg, Walter (ed.) (1988) *Neues Wörterbuch der Völkerkunde*. Reimer: Berlin.

Hofmann, Tessa (1993) *Die Armenier. Schicksal. Kultur. Geschichte*. Das Andere: Nürnberg.

Hofmann, Tessa (1997a) 'Diaspora, Migration und Sprache: Am Beispiel der Armenier in Deutschland'. In: Dum-Tragut, Jasmine (ed.) *Die armenische Sprache in der europäischen Diaspora*. Institut für Sprachwissenschaft der Universität Graz: Graz: 37-58.

Hofmann, Tessa (1997b) *Annäherung an Armenien. Geschichte und Gegenwart.* Beck'sche Reihe: München.

Hofmann, Tessa (2005) *Armenier in Berlin. Berlin und Armenien*. Der Beauftragte des Senats für Migration in Berlin: Berlin.

Ishkanian, Armine (2002) 'Mobile motherhood: Armenian women's labor migration in the post-Soviet period'. Diaspora. 11 (3): 383-415.

Kokot, Waltraud (1992) 'Kognitive Ethnologie'. In: Fischer, Hans (ed.) *Ethnologie. Einführung und Überblick*. Dietrich Reimer: Berlin, Hamburg: 367-381.

Kokot, Waltraud; Tölölyan, Khachig; Alfonso, Carolin (2004) 'Introduction'. In: Kokot, Waltraud; Tölölyan, Tölölyan; Alfonso, Carolin (eds.) *Diaspora, identity and religion. New directions in theory and research*. Routledge: London, New York: 1-8.

Kokot, Waltraud; Dorsch, Hauke (2006) *Westliche Wirtschaftsinteressen und globale Migration: Diasporen und Minderheiten in der außereuropäischen Welt. Kurseinheit 1. Diasporen in der außereuropäischen Welt – begriffliche Einordnung und inhaltliche Bestimmung*. FernUniversität in Hagen: Hagen.

Kokot, Waltraud (2007a) 'Introduction: Transformations in Thessaloniki'. In: Kokot, Waltraud (ed.) *Beyond the White Tower – Transformations in Thessaloniki. Ethnographic case studies on local aspects of urban change*. LIT: Berlin: 8-22.

Kokot, Waltraud (2007b) 'Diaspora as a resource: Transnational networks as cultural capital – factors in European integration?'. Positionpaper: http://uni.uni-hamburg.de/ethnologie/kokot.html [August 2 2008].

Kouymjian, Dickran (1997) 'Armenia from the fall of the Cilician kingdom (1375) to the forced emigration under Shah Abbas (1604)'. In: Hovannisian,

Richard G. (ed.) *The Armenian people from ancient to modern times. Volume II.* Macmillan Press LTD: London et al.: 1-50.

Lang, David Marshall; Walker, Christopher J. (1991a) 'Armenia and its history'. In: Walker, Christopher J. (ed.) *Armenia and Karabagh. The struggle for unity.* Minority Rights Group: London: 15-22.

Lang, David Marshall; Walker, Christopher J. 1(1991b) 'Armenians in the diaspora. In: Walker, Christopher J. (ed.) 'Armenia and Karabagh. The struggle for unity'. Minority Rights Group: London: 49-58.

Manaseryan, Tatoul (2004) 'Diaspora* The comparative advantage for Armenia'. Armenian International Policy Research, Working Paper No. 04/14 (January): http://pdc.ceu.hu/archive/00002659/ [March 11 2007].

Marienstras, Richard (1989) 'On the notion of diaspora'. In: Chaliand, Gérard (ed.) *Minority peoples in the age of nation-states.* Pluto Press: UK: 119-125.

Märkische Allgemeine Zeitung (21.04.2008) 'Innenausbau des Lepsius-Hauses verzögert sich'. http://www.maerkischeallgemeine.de/cms/beitrag/11187931/60709/innenausbau_des_Lepsius_Hauses_verzoegert_sich_Kreuzstein_fuer.html [May 15 2008].

Mesrobian, Arpena S. (2000) *"Like one family": The Armenians of Syracuse.* Gomidas Institute: Ann Arbor, Michigan.

Meyer, Enno (1988) 'I. Teil (bis 1922)'. In: Meyer, Enno; Berkian, Ara J. (eds.) *Zwischen Rhein und Arax. 900 Jahre deutsch-armenische Beziehungen.* Heinz Holzberg Verlag: Oldenburg: 9-92.

Meyer, Enno; Ara J. Berkian (eds.) (1988) *Zwischen Rhein und Arax. 900 Jahre deutsch-armenische Beziehungen.* Heinz Holzberg Verlag: Oldenburg.

Ministry of Foreign Affairs of Republic of Armenia (no year) 'Law of the Republic of Armenia. On citizenship of the Republic of Armenia'. www.armenia foreignministry.am/perspectives/dualcitizenship-final-eng.pdf [April 16 2008].

Mirak, Robert (1988) 'La Diaspora arménienne aux États-Unis'. Les Temps Modernes. 43 (504-506): 179-188.

Mönch, Regina (25.01.2005) 'Völkermord an den Armeniern aus dem Lehrplan genommen'. Frankfurter Allgemeine Zeitung – FAZ. 56 (20): 33.

Mönch, Regina (28.01.2005) 'Türkische Wahrheiten'. Frankfurter Allgemeine Zeitung. 56 (23): 35.

Mönch, Regina (11.02.2005) 'Schulen und Schulbuchverlage ringen mit dem Armeniergenozid'. Frankfurter Allgemeine Zeitung – FAZ. 56 (35): 35.

Mönch, Regina (21.07.2005) 'Brandenburg ist belehrbar'. Frankfurter Allgemeine Zeitung – FAZ. 56 (168): 31.

Mooradian, Karlen (1970) 'Armenian journalism. Link between East and West'. Ararat. 11 (2): 5-11.

Netzeitung.de (16.06.2005) 'Bundestag verabschiedet Armenian-Resolution'. http://www.netzeitung.de/politik/deutschland/344163.html?Bundestag_verabschiedet_Armenien-Resolution [June 30 2009].

O'Grady, Ingrid P. (1981) 'Shared meaning and choice as components of Armenian immigrant adaptation'. Anthropological Quarterly. 54 (2): 76-82.

Ordukhanyan, Azat (2005) 'Die armenischen Displaced Persons in Deutschland nach dem Zweiten Weltkrieg'. In: Drost-Abgarjan, Armenuhi; Goltz,

Hermann (eds.) *Armenologie in Deutschland. Beiträge zum Ersten Deutschen Armenologen-Tag*. LIT-Verlag: Münster: 219-232.

Oussatcheva, Marina (2001) 'Institutions in Diaspora. The case of Armenian community in Russia'. University of Oxford Transnational Communities Programme, Working Paper WPTC-01-09: http://www.transcomm.ox.ac.uk/working%20papers/WPTC-01-09%20Marina.doc.pdf [March 24 2008].

Panossian, Razmik (1998) 'Between ambivalence and intrusion: Politics and identity in Armenia-Diaspora relations'. Diaspora. 7 (2): 149-196.

Pattie, Susan Paul (1997) *Faith in history. Armenians rebuilding community*. Smithsonian Institution Press: Washington, London.

Petrosjan, Hamo (1999) 'Die Armenische Gemeinde zu Berlin (1913-1998)'. Karun. 1 (43): [n.p.].

Polm, Rita; Andrea Tauber (1997) 'Armenier/Armenierinnen'. In: Schmalz-Jacobsen, Cornelia; Hansen, Georg (eds.) *Kleines Lexikon der ethnischen Minderheiten in Deutschland*. Beck: München: 28-30.

Redgate, Anne Elizabeth (1998) *The Armenians*. Blackwell Publishers: Oxford, Malden.

Ritter, Laurence (2007) *La longue marche des Arméniens. Histoire et devenir d'une diaspora*. Robert Laffont: Paris.

Roberts, Bryan W.; Banaian, King (2004) 'Remittances in Armenia. Size, impact, and measures to enhance their contribution to development'. Task Order #PCE-I-820-98-00012-0. Report for USAID/ Armenia (October): hdr.undp.org/docs/network/hdr_net/Armenia%20Remittance%20Report.pdf [April 16 2008].

Rosenfelder, Andreas (28.07.2005) '„Wir sollen uns schämen?"'. Frankfurter Allgemeine Zeitung – FAZ. 56: (173): 29.

Safran, William (2004) 'Deconstructing and comparing diasporas'. In: Kokot, Waltraud; Tölölyan, Khachig; Alfonso, Carolin (eds.) *Diaspora, identity and religion. New directions in theory and research*. Routledge: London, New York: 9-29.

Schönwälder, Karen; Janina Söhn (2007) 'Siedlungsstrukturen von Migrantengruppen in Deutschland: Schwerpunkte der Ansiedlung und innerstädtische Konzentrationen'. Discussion paper no. SP IV 2007-601. Arbeitsstelle Interkulturelle Konflikte und gesellschaftliche Integration, Wissenschaftszentrum Berlin für Sozialforschung: Berlin: http://www.wzb.eu/zkd/aki/publications.de.htm [July 21 2008].

Schwalgin, Susanne; Martin Sökefeld (2000) 'Institutions and their agents in diaspora: A comparison of Armenians in Athens and Alevis in Germany'. WPTC-2K-11. Conference paper at the 6th European Association of Social Anthropologists Conference, Krakau: http://www.transcomm.ox.ac.uk/working_papers.htm [April 22 2007].

Schwalgin, Susanne (2004) *„Wir werden niemals vergessen!" Trauma, Erinnerung und Identität der armenischen Diaspora Griechenlands*. Transcript: Bielefeld.

Statistikamt Nord (no year) 'Zu- und Fortzüge von Armeniern in Hamburg in den Jahren 2000 bis 2007/ Einbürgerungen von Armeniern in Hamburg in den Jahren 2000 bis 2007'. Unpublished extract. Hamburg.

Statistikamt Nord (2005) 'Hamburger Stadtteil-Profile 2005'. http://fhh1.hamburg.de/fhh/behoerden/behoerde _fuer_inneres/statistisches_landesamt/profile/ [May 14 2007].

Statistische Ämter des Bundes und der Länder (29.01.2008) 'Gebiet und Bevölkerung – Fläche und Bevölkerung. 31.12.2006'. http://www.statistik-portal.de/Statistik-Portal/de_jb01_jahrtab1.asp [August 2 2008].

Statistisches Bundesamt (2006) *Strukturdaten zu Migration in Deutschland. 2004*. Statistisches Bundesamt: Wiesbaden.

Statistisches Bundesamt (2007a) *Bevölkerung und Erwerbstätigkeit. Ausländische Bevölkerung. Ergebnisse des Ausländerzentralregisters. 2006*. Fachserie 1 Reihe 2. Statistisches Bundesamt: Wiesbaden.

Statistisches Bundesamt (2007b) *Bevölkerung und Erwerbstätigkeit. Einbürgerungen. 2006*. Fachserie 1 Reihe 2.1. Statistisches Bundesamt: Wiesbaden.

Strasser, Andrea (2005) 'Globale Netzwerke – Lokale Perspektiven: Frauenrechte und deren Anwendung im armenischen Kontext'. In: Riegler, Johanna (ed.) *Kulturelle Dynamik der Globalisierung: Ost- und Westeuropäische Transformationsprozesse aus sozialanthropologischer Perspektive*. Verlag der Österreichischen Akademie der Wissenschaften: Wien: 153-173.

Talai, Vered (1986) 'Social boundaries within and between ethnic groups: Armenians in London'. MAN. The Journal of the Royal Anthropological Institute. 21 (2): 251-270.

Tauber, Andrea (1999) *Armenier in Hamburg. Ethnographie einer Gemeinde in der Diaspora*. Unpublished MA thesis. Hamburg.

Tölölyan, Khachig (1988) 'The role of the Armenian Apostolic Church in the diaspora'. The Armenian Review. 41 (1-161): 55-68.

Tölölyan, Khachig (1991) 'The nation-state and its others: In lieu of a preface'. Diaspora. 1 (1): 3-7.

Tölölyan, Khachig (1996) 'Rethinking diaspora(s): Stateless power in the transnational moment'. Diaspora. 5 (1): 3-36.

Tölölyan, Khachig (2000) 'Elites and institutions in the Armenian transnation'. Diaspora. 9 (1): 107-136.

Vertovec, Steven (1997) 'Three meanings of "diaspora," exemplified among South Asian religions'. Diaspora. 6 (3): 277-300.

Walker, Christopher (1988) 'Armenia. A nation in Asia'. Asian Affairs. Journal of the Royal Society of Asian Affairs. 19 (1): 20- 35.

Werfel, Franz (1978) *Die vierzig Tage des Musa Dagh* [1933]. Fischer: Frankfurt a. M.

Wippermann, Carsten; Flaig, Berthold Bodo (2009) 'Lebenswelten von Migrantinnen und Migranten'. Aus Politik und Zeitgeschichte. 05/2009: 3-11.

Zentralrat der Armenier in Deutschland - ZAD (no year a) 'Dokumente'. http://www.d-armenier.de/cms/html/modules.php?op=modload&name=Downloads&file=index [May 21 2008].

Zentralrat der Armenier in Deutschland - ZAD (no year b) 'Über uns'. http://www.d-armenier.de/cms/html/index.php?module=pagesetter&tid=15 [March 21 2008].

lines

Beiträge zur Stadtforschung aus dem Institut für Ethnologie der Universität Hamburg
hrsg. von Prof. Dr. Waltraud Kokot

Laura von Bierbrauer
Recuperadores Urbanos
Abfallsammeln als Überlebensstrategie auf den Straßen von Buenos Aires
Bd. 5, 2012, 136 S., 19,90 €, br., ISBN 978-3-643-11088-6

Astrid Wonneberger (Ed.)
Cultural Contrasts in Dublin
A montage of ethnographic studies
Up to the 1990s, Dublin and Irish urban cultures had only been marginally studied by cultural and social anthropologists, even though the Greater Dublin Area has been home to almost one third of the Republic's population for several decades. From this time anthropologists slowly became aware of the variety of cultural groups and topics which shape Ireland's capital.
This growing awareness went hand in hand with the major economic, architectural, social and cultural changes which Dublin was experiencing. Sparked by Ireland's membership of the EU (then EEC) and accelerated by the Celtic Tiger economy and increasing numbers of immigrants, the city has turned into a multicultural space of a variety unprecedented before.
The articles in this book are based on a student research project in Dublin in 2006, presenting four ethnographic case studies ranging from immigra-

LIT Verlag Berlin – Münster – Wien – Zürich – London
Auslieferung Deutschland / Österreich / Schweiz: siehe Impressumsseite